THE LEWIS LETTERS

The Exploits of a 20th Century Aviator and Adventurer

PAM MCKENZIE

To Lorne my boss!
Pam McKenzie
Nov 2017

◆ FriesenPress

Suite 300 - 990 Fort St
Victoria, BC, V8V 3K2
Canada

www.friesenpress.com

Copyright © 2017 by Pam McKenzie
First Edition — 2017

All rights reserved.

Photograph of Pam McKenzie is credited to Jana Wenzel.

No part of this publication may be reproduced in any form, or by any means, electronic or mechanical, including photocopying, recording, or any information browsing, storage, or retrieval system, without permission in writing from FriesenPress.

ISBN
978-1-5255-1112-7 (Hardcover)
978-1-5255-1113-4 (Paperback)
978-1-5255-1114-1 (eBook)

1. TRANSPORTATION, AVIATION, HISTORY

Distributed to the trade by The Ingram Book Company

CONTENTS

Part One   **7**
WWI and the Early Years, Pre–1924   9

Part Two   **33**
The Hudson Strait Expedition 1927–28   39
A Forced Landing on the Ice Floes   57
Northwards up the Labrador Coast to Port Burwell   77

Part Three   **101**
Epilogue   111
Endnotes/References   115

Acknowledgements

IN THE PAST few months, it has been my privilege to examine the letters, diaries and pictures of Mr. Alexander Lewis, as entrusted to the Royal Aviation Museum of Western Canada, by his godson, Mr. Kelly Jones.

In my research, a fascinating story came to light, several in fact. The WWI adventures of a young eighteen-year-old pilot over the front lines in France, a first-hand account of the Kilmichael Ambush in Northern Ireland, the diary of the pilot from the Hudson Strait Expedition that crashed on the ice in the North Atlantic and walked for thirteen days to survive. A lifetime of survival and service, all in his own words …

This is history worth remembering. And truly stories worth telling once again.

Thank you to the wonderful volunteers of the museum Library and Archives who catalogued, scanned, proofed and encouraged me along the way. I am so grateful for your time and talents; it was a pleasure to know and work with you all.

And mostly, thank you Kelly Jones for sharing the amazing story of your godfather with all of us.

Pam McKenzie
July 2017

PART ONE

WWI and the Early Years, Pre–1924

ALEXANDER LEWIS WAS born on July 15, 1899 in Fishponds, Bristol, England. Throughout his lifetime, he was an active participant in the seminal events of the twentieth century. From the skies over the front lines of WWI Europe, to the frozen icefields of Hudson Strait, to the cold waters of the North Atlantic in WWII, his is a story worth telling and a history worth remembering. Through the impressive collection in the Archives of the Royal Aviation Museum of Western Canada, the storied life of Alexander Lewis lives on.

> The following are excerpts from autobiographical notes and correspondence, *in his own words exactly as written, with corrections for spelling and punctuation.*

Part One

I WAS BORN and grew up almost in the shadow of the Graham White Aviation Company's factory and aerodrome at Filton in the beautiful Gloucestershire country in England. Flying was therefore in my blood. In those early days of 1909 and on as a little boy of nine or thereabouts, I would take my bicycle and spend the entire day outside the fence around the aerodrome in the hope that an aeroplane would fly. When I was fourteen I was lucky enough to get a flight in an old Blériot monoplane out of that aerodrome and that convinced me where my future career lay, much to the consternation of my people who considered my decision as a form of suicide. In those days, circa 1909, anyone who wanted to fly was considered to be an ideal candidate for the lunatic asylum.

My school days were rather protected ones in that I was sent to the Irish Christian Brothers College (St. Brendan's) in Bristol. My parents were devout Catholics and nursed the fervent hope that one day I would be a Catholic priest … My ambition however was somewhat different and in due course I matriculated to the Bristol University.

At this time, the First World War was on and all those undergrads who were medically fit automatically joined the Officers' Training Corps. One fine day when we were on parade a senior officer for London appeared and addressing the parade asked for volunteers for the Royal Flying Corps. Five of us volunteered and were accepted. I was exactly seventeen years and four months old and received my pilot's wings and commission as a 2nd Lieutenant before I was eighteen.

I was slated to go to France as a fighter pilot but there was an urgent call for R.E.8 pilots on the Ypres-Passchendaele front where there had been a terrific number of two-seaters shot down by the Richthofen circus so I was posted to that front. I was also shot down by seven Fokker D7s within the first month. I was fortunate to get down our side of the lines partially out of control but with enough to survive and return to the squadron where I remained until the armistice in November 1918.

Letters Home

The Lewis Letters

WWI Letters Home (All with salutation My Dear Mother)

Sept 2, 1917 — Cadet A. Lewis — South Farnboro, UK

Thank you so very much for your parcel but not having opened it yet as the tent is crowded (11 in the tent)…I believe I told you we had three returned cadets in our tent, well if ever I have seen anybody so fed up before it is them. At Winchester they had everything served up in style, waitresses to wait on them, tablecloths, cups and saucers, flowers on the tables, and of course they were treated as gentlemen, and then to be returned to this hovel here.

… (T)hey are turning them down wholesale now at the medical examinations, about three weeks ago they were accepting anybody, in fact some of the cadets say that the RFC now is only a trap to get chaps for the infantry … 50 cadets were returned on Saturday evening … about two hours afterwards another 40 cadets came in returned …

Nov 27, 1917 — Cadet A. Lewis — St Leonards-on-Sea, Sussex

Hastings is only 40 to 50 miles from Ostend, I haven't listened for them but I am told that one can hear the guns in France quite well. It hardly seems right that I am so much nearer France than home.

March 2, 1918 — 2 Lt. A. Lewis — Stamford, Lincshire

We have not been able to do any flying today because of the wind. The wind is simply fearful and so very cold, yesterday and today it has been snowing so you can tell what it is like in a large aerodrome during that weather, right out in the midst of the country …

I received my cheque … yesterday, I have £71.9.0 credited to me, £31.9.0 for two months' pay and £41.0.0 for my outfit allowance, of course it should be £50, but they deducted £9 for my outfit which I had when I was a cadet.

June 20, 1918 — Artillery Co-operation School, Nr. Winchester, Hants

I have a batman who cleans all of my stuff, makes my bed, etc. The other chap in the tent is a Lieutenant in the Canadian Artillery who will eventually be an observer.

We have all lady motor-drivers and also a great many lady mechanics who get the machines ready for flight, etc.

I shall be here about a fortnight or three weeks there being sufficient pilots in France at the present time.

July 6, 1918 — Worthy Down Aerodrome, Nr. Winchester, Hants

One of our chaps nose-dived to the ground from 1,500 feet in an R.E.8. An old farmer over 70 years of age who happened to be in the same field, rushed up and pulled him out of the wreckage, just in time to save him from being burnt to death. The farmer was burned about the arms and the pilot died in the hospital the next day, awfully plucky of the farmer though.

July 20, 1918   —   Worthy Down Aerodrome, Nr. Winchester, Hants

The papers are looking a trifle better the last two or three days. Yesterday, the Germans were pushed back eight miles. We get all these news straight from the front. You see we have a wireless station on the aerodrome which catches every wireless message of every description whether sent from Germany or France. We get the German Official report in German, from Berlin every morning at 11:00 a.m. and it is jolly interesting having it translated and hearing Germany's secrets. We also get the Paris Official report every afternoon at 4:00 p.m., which is the report you generally read in the stop-press of the evening papers.

When I am back in civil life I should very much like to have wireless apparatus set up on the top of the house, it would be awfully interesting.

Aug 7, 1918   —   Worthy Down Aerodrome, Nr. Winchester, Hants

Hall, the transport officer had an earwig crawl into his ear last night. He nearly went mad and had to be taken to hospital in a car in the middle of the night. By syringing, they were able to kill it but they couldn't get it out, the doctor spent two hours trying to get it out, but couldn't, he is trying again tonight. The funny part of it is, he left his tent because of the earwigs, and went to sleep in a hut and it was in the hut that the earwig crawled into his ear.

Aug 11, 1918   —   Lieut. A. Lewis   —   No 2 Air Supply Depot, RAF BEF, France

I am at last in France … I had to ride 45 kilometres about 40 miles in a Leyland lorry and thoroughly enjoyed it … it was awfully interesting riding … in an open lorry through French country passing through curious little French villages.

When we were crossing the channel, an airship which was escorting us over, blew up by means of his machine guns two enemy mines, they made a terrific row.

By the papers, we have captured 3,500 prisoners and 500 officers so I guess the war will not be very long about now, it is only a matter of time, the Germans cannot hold out against America's fresh and numerous troops.

Aug 12, 1918 — No 2 Air Supply Depot, RAF BEF, France

We are also quite near to a certain large French town which you would sure to know quite well, if I were only permitted to disclose the name of it to you.

There is a certain little village here in which are some large dumps and hospitals, Hun aeroplanes come over nearly every night and strafe them like fury. We have quite an exciting time.

Aug 16, 1918 — No 7 Squadron, RAF, BEF, France

As you can see by above, I have again changed my address, I am now only three or four miles from the line, and having a topping time. All day long, you can hear the guns bellowing and at night the flashes are like lightning flashes, except that they last longer.

The Hun machines are over nearly every night trying to bomb our aerodrome, but they have never succeeded yet. They drop bombs all around but never on it.

A dirty skunk of a Hun has been flying around in one of our machines and shot down two of ours, up to now he has been pretty sporty in the air; but this spoils it all.

Aug 18, 1918 — No 7 Squadron, RAF, BEF, France

I went up this morning about 10:00 a.m. but it was frightfully bumpy and windy. Our part of the front is very quiet at present but the Hun is pretty lively in the air, now. He never attacks singly, always in circuses of about five or six.

Although we are so near the line we are extremely comfortable … We get any amount of food out there, as much as we can eat, and ripping food too. We always get plenty of real cream for dessert (not ideal milk but real stuff).

Aug 19, 1918 — No 7 Squadron, RAF, BEF, France

I have just returned from a flip over the lines. On my way I happened to look down and saw a large town simply a mass of ruins. It had a church right in the middle or rather the remains of a church, it did seem an awful shame. I wish I could tell you the name, but I must not, although you have read about it enough in the papers, when you see things like that, it makes you long to do something similar to the Hun in return.

This is now 4:30 p.m., I am off over the lines again at 6:30. We meet very few Hun machines and those we do meet, run away and fire from a distance. I always thought better of the Huns than that. It only goes to prove that he is well aware of the fact that we have predominance in the air, and what is more, we mean to keep it.

We are having pretty decent weather, although rather gusty and cloudy. When I was flying over the trenches today, I pitied the poor bounders inside and compared them with our nice, little, comfortable huts, there is no doubt about it, the RAF is the force now, I should strongly recommend anyone contemplating joining the army, to join the RAF.

Aug 20, 1918 — No 7 Squadron, RAF, BEF, France

Yesterday evening I was over the line for two hours 25 minutes, I saw some action, etc., but some scout machines, which happened to be above us, kept the Hun machines off. When I say us I mean my observer and myself.

We have quite a number of mascots here, two goats, one of which is just cutting his horns so therefore, every rotten hard thing he comes in contact with is used by him for rubbing his head. It is very amusing although it must be rather painful for him. We also have two little tiny pups, pretty little things whose sole object in life seems to be in chasing the neighbouring rats who have taken up quarters around about our huts, but who, luckily for us, never try to ingratiate themselves any further.

Aug 21, 1918 — No 7 Squadron, RAF, BEF, France

I was over Hunland for three hours today dropping bombs. The Huns were firing off anti-aircraft guns at me like fury, they all burst around me but never hit me. You see, they could not get the proper range because I kept stunting and therefore I was never in the same place twice, there were also a lot of Hun machines around but they were busy with some other of our machines, so I was not disturbed by them.

Aug 24, 1918 — No 7 Squadron, RAF, BEF, France

We have had it rather rainy today but I expect it will clear up by this evening when I have to make a trip over Hunland and do something to get the nuisance of a war over …

You ought to see our padre, the protestant chaplain, he plays cards for money, plays every kind of games, takes joyrides as a passenger in our busses and is a regular sport. What makes it all the more amusing is that he looks exactly like a clergyman with a long face, and long hair parted down the middle, big blue eyes and a long pointed nose.

Aug 25, 1918 — No 7 Squadron, RAF, BEF, France

This afternoon I took a captain in the infantry up for a flip. It was the first time he had ever been in a plane. I had him up for three quarters of an hour. When he came down, he never seemed to weary of thanking me, in fact he has proffered me an invitation to visit him at his headquarters about six miles away.

Aug 26, 1918 — No 7 Squadron, RAF, BEF, France

… (O)f course the war may last for quite a long time yet, but as things are going at present the war should be over in a very short time and if they continue as they are doing now, the war <u>will</u> be over in a very short time. We, in the Air Force see and know more than most branches of the service. In the air we can see the actual battles raging and also see the turn of the tide which, ever since I have been out here has been on our side; that is without any exaggeration whatever.

Aug 27, 1918 — No 7 Squadron, RAF, BEF, France

I took up another infantry officer for his first joy-flip this morning, and took him over his camp where he is stationed. I flew over it at an extremely low altitude whilst he dropped a note weighted by means of a stone in the envelope. He was quite elated.

Sept 4, 1918 — No 7 Squadron, RAF, BEF, France

Yesterday afternoon, I with three others went on a long bombing raid bombing a certain Hun town. Somehow or other I got separated from the others owing to clouds so therefore had to beetle along all on my own. I got over this certain Hun town, circled around it two or three times and then dropped my bombs, which as soon as they reached the ground caused several fires. As soon as I had dropped my bombs, up came the anti-aircraft guns at me. I have never had such close shaves in all my life before. One burst right on my wingtip, another nearly on my tail, and in fact all around me. I had to stunt like fury in order to mislead their gunners. The sky around me was literally black with the shells exploding. My observer had colossal wind-up, but nevertheless I managed to drop my bombs and get back safely which was the … thing.

Just this minute heard we have captured Lens with 10,000 prisoners. War will be over by Christmas.

Sept 7, 1918 — No 7 Squadron, RAF, BEF, France

Yesterday morning, I took an American Captain up for a flip. In return he gave me the use of his motorcycle and sidecar. it was a large six-horse Clyno Combination and, by jove, it could move. I took my observer in the sidecar and went a deuce of a way, it was almost like a car to drive, clutch, three gears etc.

Lewis, left, with unidentified companion, somewhere on the Western Front in France

Sept 11, 1918 — No 7 Squadron, RAF, BEF, France

We have been doing very little flying lately because of the rain. It has been raining now continuously for three days. Today I got fed up with doing nothing so I got a Crossley tender and went right up to the front line, or rather where the front line was just before the Germans retreated. I spent the afternoon exploring a large town, which was held by the Germans a few days ago. It was simply a mass of ruins. I went into the ruins of several large chateaux, which used to be owned by counts and people like that. It seemed a horrible shame, all the walls were gilded, large oak doors, beautiful massive furniture, splendid oil paintings, beautiful staircases, etc. Everything was ruined but not so much that you couldn't see what it used to be like. There were three tremendous cupboards in one chateau filled with splendid crockery, gold and silver dishes and every type of glass drinking vessel you can imagine. Everything was smashed to bits.

All the roads were simply full of deep shell holes, with dead horses, etc. lying by the side of the road. There wasn't one single house or outhouse left standing. I was just wondering as I was walking among the ruins how many dead bodies those piles of fallen bricks hid.

Sept 12, 1918 — No 7 Squadron, RAF, BEF, France

We are still having rotten weather, raining all the time and awfully cold, but I do not mind, we are a hundred times better off than the chaps in the trenches, with our huts, complete with beds, etc., every convenience and batmen to do everything for us and when we are flying it is so exciting fighting Hun machines and dodging Archies that we consider it almost like playing a game of draughts seeing who can out-do the other. You see, in the air, if we let a Hun get on our tail we are almost as good as dead men, the same implies to him. You see, when a Hun is on our tail we can't plug him with our machine guns because if we did, we should shoot our own tail off, so that he can fire at us as much as he likes, but I assure you we seldom let that happen.

I have been out here now over a month, it is said that if we survive the first month we are good for the rest of the months, it is generally only newcomers that go under.

Sept 20, 1918   —   No 7 Squadron, RAF, BEF, France

I have been feeling absolutely up the … yesterday and today. You see, yesterday a very great friend of mine was killed. He was an observer, lived in the same hut with me and shared the same batman. He went up yesterday about 11:30 a.m. with a new pilot to do a job of work over the lines. At 12:30 news came through that the pilot had lost control and the machine had nose-dived to the ground, both being instantly killed. The engine could not be seen, it was right in the ground.

I was due to go up at one and I can assure you, I did not feel like it, but I went up. I was flying over Hunland a little later when I suddenly saw one of our observation balloons burst into flames and fall to the ground; immediately after, I saw a Hun machine diving straight for us. I let him come on until he was nearly on us, then I split-essed[1] around so that he had passed us before he knew where he was. I immediately split-essed around again and dived right on him while my observer emptied the contents of his Lewis machine gun into him. That settled him, he dived right into the ground, so that is how my observer and I got our first Hun down.

I was one of the bearers yesterday at the funeral of the pilot and observer spoken of, they were buried at a little Canadian Casualty Station not far from our drome. There were no coffins, the remains were put in sacks and over each grave will be placed a propeller cut out in the form of a cross with a brass plate … bearing the inscription.

Sept 22, 1918   —   No 7 Squadron, RAF, BEF, France

Misfortunes never come single handed. Another pilot and observer of ours were attacked by five Huns and brought down in flames but what can you expect when it is five to one.

The Huns were over last night trying to bomb our aerodrome, one bomb fell about a hundred yards away from my hut blowing out all the candles, blowing open the doors, windows, etc. and

---

1   The Split S or Split-S is a manoeuvre taught for use in dogfighting, when the pilot has the opportunity to withdraw from an air battle. The aircraft is rolled inverted and pulled through in a half-loop.

making a terrible noise. I was in bed asleep at the time when I was suddenly awakened by the above commotion. I thought the end of the world had come.

Sept 29, 1918   —   No 7 Squadron, RAF, BEF, France

I expect you are wondering why I have not written before, but the news in the papers will tell you the reason why. Isn't it ripping and they have not finished pushing yet?

I have been in the push right from the beginning and have been extremely lucky, not having, up to now, come to any grief. There used to be two Catholic officers with whom I used to go to church, one of them is killed, the other wounded, so I have to go to church by myself now. We have lost quite a number the last two days, the night after the first day of the push, our mess seemed quite empty, but the Huns have lost a great many more, they are being beaten on all fronts now, so peace is not so very far away.

We are flying in all kinds of weather now; this afternoon I was flying in the pouring rain. A very curious incident happened yesterday, one of our planes was attacked by nine Hun machines, and was forced to land in Hunland, the pilot being wounded and the observer killed. Of course they were taken prisoners. The same afternoon we made an attack and captured that part of land in which they were, the pilot is now in our hands again. The day before, this pilot and myself had each taken up an infantry officer for a joyride. These infantry officers invited us to dinner the following day but naturally the above incident prevented the appointment from being kept.

Oct 1, 1918   —   No 7 Squadron, RAF, BEF, France

… I paid a visit to the front line and had quite an interesting, if uncomfortable time.

I made a tour of the German dug-outs, evacuated by them two or three days ago, during our great push. I came across one with a beautiful German machine gun well-oiled and greased, not rusty at all. The German machine-gunner must have taken to his hills and run away leaving everything behind. Of course I couldn't take the machine gun away, it being too heavy but I took a bayonet that was lying by the side of it.

During my walk around, or rather, wade around, I encountered an awful smell, then I suddenly perceived all around me a lot of human bones, leg bones, arm bones, breast bones, etc. It quite put the wind up me! Looking closer I saw that it had been formerly a graveyard, which had been laid open disclosing all of the bodies, by the various shells falling on it. There were also a lot of swells with piles of lead coffins burst open floating in water; it was a most gruesome sight.

The country all around is simply a mass of desolation, not a house to be seen, here and there an isolated tree stump, at one time, probably forming part of a wood or forest. Wherever you walk you have to step in and out deep shell craters filled with water. It makes one feel horribly lonely and yet, in spite of the fact that not a single soul can be seen, there are really thousands of troops dug into the ground trying to make themselves comfortable in muddy dug-outs literally teaming with rats and other such vermin, trenches full of water, etc., and yet this is only the least of what they have to go through.

I commenced this letter yesterday. This morning very early I was over a certain Hun town dropping bombs, the Hun anti-aircraft guns were exceedingly busy throwing up a perfect barrage all around me but luckily not hitting me, I was looking over the side of the plane seeing where my bombs hit when suddenly without any warning I heard the frop-frop-frop of machine guns right on top of me, at the same time my machine lurched and the nose dropped. I looked around and saw seven Fokkers right on me. Their leader was diving right on my tail and seemed to be surrounded in a mass of smoke, which formed a kind of star-shape around the front of his machine. The smoke came from his machine guns, which he was firing like stink at me. He looked a splendid sight but there was no time to think of that. I split-essed around firing at them at grim death not thinking for a moment that I should ever drive them off because there were seven of them against one, myself. Anyhow I must have put the wind up them with the machine gun for instead of coming on me in one straight dive regardless of my machine gun bullets, they would dive at me, then when

I fired they would bank away. They dived at me four separate times and riddled my machine with bullets, then beetled off altogether. It is the nearest shave I have ever had, seven on to one is no joke especially when not another of our machines could be seen in the sky.

I managed to crab the machine somehow or other back to our aerodrome and finally landed. The tail plane was simply riddled with bullet holes and the wires shot away. It is a miracle how I ever came out of it. I had a new observer who had only been over the lines three times before so he had a good christening.

Oct 6, 1918 — No 7 Squadron, RAF, BEF, France

Owing to the great number of casualties we have had lately, I happen to be the senior flying officer in our flight. It is remarkable the number of changes we have had in so short a time.

I was at church again this morning and was surprised to see that the left wing in which the … altar used to be, was absolutely destroyed. The Huns have been shelling us quite a lot lately but they haven't touched our drome yet.

Oct 16, 1918 — No 7 Squadron, RAF, BEF, France

We have advanced so far on our part of the front that now, our aerodrome is fifty miles away from the line. It takes a half an hour to fly to the line now, whereas before it took a few minutes although in a few days we are taking possession of a Hun aerodrome not far from the present front line.

When I was attacked by those Fokkers, it was not exactly my observer's fault, although perhaps it was in a way. You see, I was dropping bombs on a certain Hun town and we were both hanging over the side looking to see where they dropped. It is awfully interesting dropping bombs. You first release a bomb then watch it falling down until it strikes the roof of a house. Then you see an enormous burst of yellow flame and smoke, which gradually dies down until you see a few ruins smoldering with a few flames knocking around. Then you fly on a little farther and do it in like manner.

Oct 27, 1918 — No 7 Squadron, RAF, BEF, France

You are doubtless wondering why I have not written for such a long time but we have been so busy driving the Bosch over the Rhine that there has been very little time to settle down to do any letter writing.

Of course we have moved our aerodrome further up as the line advances and are now only about five miles away from the line but I can assure you that will not be for very long. We are at present in a Hun aerodrome evacuated by them a few days before we took possession and quite an elaborate affair it is, wooden hangars with concrete floors and quite a large field for taking off and landing in.

Nov 23, 1918 — No 7 Squadron, RAF, BEF, France

We are one of the squadrons that has to follow up our advancing troops and so therefore we shall be on the move practically all the time and will have to stay in Germany for several months after peace is declared.

We are moving away from here in about three days' time so shall see some more life. This morning, I flew right over Brussels, circled around it and returned; it was a deuce of a way away from the drome, thought I was never getting there.

Dec 9, 1918 — No 7 Squadron, RAF, BEF, France

I have at last arrived in Germany, we flew over yesterday … starting at 2:00 p.m. and arriving here at 3:45 p.m. As far as I can see at present Germany is a beautiful place, nothing else but hills and dales but extremely cold. We were speaking to some Huns yesterday who told us that we must have brought the English weather along with us for generally about this time of year there are three feet of snow and umpteen degrees of frost.

We are stationed at a place called Eisenbahn Camp, which is nothing more or less than a tremendous Hun barracks, a peacetime one, holding about 25,000 men, when we took it over there were 5,000 Hun recruits in training here. It really is a beautiful place, right in the heart of a large fine forest, but miles and miles away from any town or village. To make up for that there are barber shops and canteens all over the place still kept by the original German people. Our aerodrome is a large field about three kilometres away from the camp on which are no hangars or anything not having been used for an aerodrome before so our machines are naturally exposed to all winds and weather. But of course we are not staying here long, only a matter of a few days when we shall be moving further still into Germany.

It was a beautiful flip over yesterday, before starting off we got to a height of 3,000 feet over Namur but when we came to the Ardennes Mountains, which of course we had to fly over to reach Germany we found we were only about 1,000 feet, it was a very curious sight. France and Belgium was a mass of sunlight whilst the mountains and Germany were dark and overcast with clouds. It was quite warm when we took off at Namur but on landing in Germany we found it raw, foggy and cold.

I have been driving a Crossley car quite a lot the last three or four days. We are awfully short of drivers so the C.O. asked if there were any officers who could drive a car. I immediately said that I could, so I was driving it until we left Namur. I did enjoy myself. You see, before all of the driving I did was unofficial because officers were not supposed to drive a government car, that being considered a chauffeur's job.[2]

After the War

ALEXANDER LEWIS RECORDED *in his autobiographical notes that:*
After the peace treaty was signed we flew our squadron back to England and shortly after we were demobilized back into civilian life. I was too unsettled to return to university with the horrors and

---

2   This was the last surviving letter from WWI.

nightmares still fresh in my mind of the air war on the Ypres front. We were over enemy territory every day and sometimes at night, sitting ducks with our obsolete R.E.8s for any type of enemy aircraft that happened to be around, and through the appalling weather of a Flanders winter.

Air Ministry License, 14 July 1920

After the war, I obtained my Air Ministry commercial flying license and barn-stormed all over England giving joyrides at a half-guinea a time in Avro 504Ks converted to three-seaters, also charter trips to points in Europe. I was on the Reserve of Officers and did my annual training on the latest types of Air Force aircraft from time to time. I also got a job with a Flying Boat company … incidentally I was a partner in this company but owing to tremendous overhead expenses and a paucity of customers as a result of the current depression the company was forced to close down and I lost all my investment.

Shortly after this episode I was at home in Bristol and was reading the *Sunday Pictorial* when I came across a cryptic request from Scotland Yard headquarters in London that they would be pleased to hear from ex-officers to join the special branch for a very special assignment. This was right up my alley so on Monday morning I caught the nine o'clock train to Paddington and took a taxi to Scotland Yard. I still remember the strange look the taxi driver gave me for I was still quite young and of course he took me for a Scotland Yard detective, which eventually I turned out to be.

Arriving at Scotland Yard, I was taken down innumerable passages and several flights of stairs to a huge long room at the end of which was a large desk and sitting behind it the Commissioner in charge of the Special Branch. Without wasting any time, he looked at my identification papers and then picked up the phone and called the Air Ministry to confirm everything I had told him. Having received due confirmation, he then outlined the new policy that the Prime Minister of England David Lloyd George had ordered Scotland Yard to implement. This policy was to take over the complete policing of the whole of Southern Ireland, which was then in a state of turmoil with wholesale murders taking place almost daily of Army personnel and the permanent members of the Royal Irish Constabulary. The idea was to create an alternate reign of terror and to beat the Sinn-Fein and the Irish Republican Army at their own game. I accepted the challenge whereupon I was immediately sworn in and because I was an ex-officer was given the temporary rank of Police Sergeant to be confirmed in six months' time. To cut a long story short I served in the R.I.C. for a number of years and attained the rank of Inspector. Eventually of course the Republic of Ireland came into being and the R.I.C. was disbanded.

My years in Southern Ireland were fraught with many horrors and terrific hard work including undercover work to ferret out the rebels and their arms and ammunition. During this period, I received the dubious distinction of being the No. 1 on the blacklist of the I.R.A. for immediate execution if captured, as a result of some very successful raids and captures resulting in the deaths of some of their most prominent leaders.

When I was stationed in Cork (there were only 37 of us altogether) and of that small number 18 were murdered in an ambush one Sunday night by over 200 of the I.R.A. I was one of the remaining 19 who found the bodies on Monday morning horribly mutilated on a lonely peat bog road with the police cars blown up and burned. My experiences in Ireland would fill a book and I was suffering nightmares for more years after.

Dec 17, 1920 — Macroom Castle, Macroom, Co. Cork

My Dear Mother,

In answer to yours just received, as you say, things are still pretty lively over here, but I have now reached that stage that I don't care a hang what happens; things that a month ago would have shocked me have ceased to affect me in the same manner. I can now kill a Sinn Feiner in quite a casual, conscientious way. To you, it may seem a horrid thing to say, but if you had only seen a quarter of what I had seen, you would quite understand.

In your last letter … you say how horrible it must have been for me to have <u>seen</u> our fellows <u>brought in</u> from the ambush. It was I who had to go out and <u>bring them in</u>; we were the relief party. On the Sunday afternoon, old Craig with whom I had been dining the previous evening, took out two cars for a patrol. That afternoon I was fitting a new petrol tank on to my bus … otherwise I should also have been on that fatal patrol. I had been on that same road three times with Craig the same week, so Guthrie who was also driving a car took his instead. They should have been back at seven o'clock at the latest. They did not arrive that night so the next morning the C.O. came up to me and asked me to get my car out saying that we had better go and try and find out what had happened to them. We both thought that they had perhaps had a breakdown. We set out and had covered about ten miles when travelling along the Kilmichael Road I suddenly noticed a Crossley tender absolutely burnt out, lying in the ditch on the left hand side of the road. A few yards further on I saw a dead body, which happened to be poor old Barnes, lying on its back in a pool of blood. About a hundred yards down the road was the other Crossley, also burnt out, also in the left hand ditch, and around which were all the other dead bodies. At that every one of us went raving mad. I took two petrol cans, went to the nearest farmhouse, out of which all the occupants had fled, emptied the contents all over the place, down the stairs, over the bedding etc. and put a light to the lot, it went up with a roar and that was the finish of that. The others did likewise to another farmhouse and haystack close by.

When we had cooled down a bit we proceeded to pick up the bodies and pile them in the tender, then commenced an awful return home. I had my car filled with mutilated corpses while the others walked in front. I have never driven a more gruesome load before and never wish to again. On arriving back at the castle, we deposited our awful burden and went to the nearest undertakers to order sixteen coffins, which we called for about two hours later. The rest needs no explanation; do you wonder that I am longing to be back again in Fishpond if only for a fortnight? As a matter of fact, I nearly succeeded in getting home for Christmas but as so many of our people are resigning, quite a number have sent in their resignations since the ambush, I have had to forfeit it … I was quite looking forward to being home for Christmas, but never mind, I will enjoy it just as well afterwards. Of course, it is being granted me more as a nerve steadier than anything else, otherwise I shouldn't have been home for ages.

Palestine

WE HAD BEEN promised a position for life and after we left Ireland those of us who were lucky to survive were sent to the Middle East to Palestine to form the British Palestine Gendarmerie for the express purpose of enforcing the Balfour Declaration [November 2, 1917] giving the mandate of Palestine to the Jews; an insidious decision and an insult to democracy inasmuch as the Arabs formed over two-thirds of the population. After Ireland, Palestine was a picnic; we were the police and our job was to keep peace between the Arabs and the Jews, there were a few exciting incidents but it was too monotonous a life for me, so after fifteen months I resigned and made my way to Port Said, and boarded a Japanese ship for England.

Jan 1, 1923 — British Gendarmerie, Nazareth, Palestine
My Dear Mother,

I have had a ripping Christmas, one of the best I have ever had, I believe, because you see I spent it in Bethlehem and Jerusalem. Jerusalem is just over a hundred miles from Nazareth and Bethlehem is only ten miles from Jerusalem … [lengthy description of visiting the Church of the Nativity, the Church of the Holy Sepulcher, Mount Calvary, the Mount of Olives and the Dead Sea] … and now comes the most magnificent sight I have ever seen and that is a statue of Our Blessed Virgin covered with jewels, diamonds, precious stones of every description, rings and other valuables worth over three million pounds, there is one ruby alone which costs £20,000. There is a present there from every crowned head in the world of this generation and of many generations past, a most magnificent sight.

Jerusalem is a very interesting town with quite a number of Europeans. The Jaffa Gate is rather famous, the real gate wasn't big enough for the Kaiser's car to get through so he issued orders that a bigger gap should be made in the town wall, which incidentally is ninety feet thick so accordingly it was done and has quite spoilt the old traditions of the spot.

Then of course, we had to come to earth again when we arrived back here and be perfectly good sergeants. Needless to say we shall all be on the boat again as soon as the contract is finished; it is getting more unbearable every day. Fifty per cent of the chaps are Irishmen and as soon as each side gets a drop of whiskey into them, there is a battle royal for then their true nature comes to the top and their hatred of Englishmen is simply colossal. The worst of it is there is no fighting out here for it is then the Englishman comes out on top and the Irishman is a born coward.

Back Home in England

I RENEWED MY commercial flying license, also the engine, aircraft and instrument licenses and was able to carry out my Reserve Officers training on the latest types at the Bristol Aeroplane factory aerodrome at Filton. The chief pilot there was an old friend of mine … and he kept me on for the odd bit of test flying such as endurance flying and height tests on the few types of aircraft they were manufacturing and reconditioning during that period of the aviation doldrums.

    The year was 1924, a time of depression in England and I couldn't foresee any future in flying for some time to come so I decided to come to Canada and review the situation there, so I booked a passage on the good ship *Melita* and sailed out of Southampton for the New World …

    To Be Continued … *with the Hudson Strait Expedition crash [an international news event of its day] and Group Captain Alexander Lewis's meritorious WWII service and beyond.*

Pam McKenzie

PART TWO

All quotes are from the diaries of Alexander Lewis in his own words, with corrections for spelling and punctuation.

The New World

ON ARRIVAL AT Quebec, I took the train for Montreal and found some excellent lodgings in Westmount. I proceeded to write letters all over the place, and received four offers of employment as a pilot. One was from the Canadian Air Board, asking me to go to Ottawa for an interview, as I already held a commission in the RAF Reserve of Officers, a commercial pilot's license and other engineering licenses.

In due course, I arrived in Ottawa and was interviewed by Group Captain Scott, Director of the Canadian Air Board. This was Dec 1924 and the Canadian Air Force was about to come into being. We were still wearing the old dark blue uniform with silver pips and wings. To cut a long story short, I was accepted and thus my RCAF service commenced.

I must confess that I found it most difficult to adjust. At the age of twenty-five, I was a veteran of World War I, the Royal Irish Constabulary and the British Palestine Gendarmerie. I had held commissioned rank in all these services and had had responsibilities involving matters of life and death for those under my command. Reporting to Camp Borden was like entering the Garden of Eden.

Camp Borden

Alexander Lewis, nicknamed Jaggs, on the completion of his training in Camp Borden, was stationed in Winnipeg. He there met Jeanette Cady and on June 25, 1927 they married. On July 15, 1927, a scant three weeks later, Alexander Lewis leaves as part of the Hudson Strait Expedition.

He is not to return for one full year. And is presumed dead …

The Hudson Strait Expedition 1927–28

The Genesis

THE HUDSON STRAIT is a 500-mile-long channel of stormy, ice-choked sea that separates Baffin Island from the Labrador mainland. Remote and inaccessible, this area was considered fraught with dangers and hardships for any hardy adventurers who dared intrude into its icy fastness. Faced with contradictory information on the length of time the Strait could be navigated, in 1927 the Government of Canada commissioned an expedition with the Departments of Marine and Fisheries, Railways and Defence.

In the early spring of that year, the Hudson Strait Expedition was organized to determine the maximum length of time during the summer months in which the Hudson Strait was sufficiently clear of ice to permit ocean-going ships … to pass through for the transportation of grain from Winnipeg via Churchill to the ports of Europe … By carrying out daily air patrols continuously as weather permitted for one entire winter and summer, these comprehensive findings would determine exactly the earliest possible opening date and last possible closing date with a reasonable factor of safety to shipping.

This was not a simple undertaking. The plan called for three bases to be built, one at each end of the Hudson Strait and one halfway between. Each base was to have two aircraft and a high-power radio station, built to broadcast daily the findings of the aircraft patrols direct to Ottawa along with local meteorological readings. The expedition would require … the erection of suitable dwellings that could withstand the rigors of an Arctic winter and winds of hurricane proportions for which the Strait is famous, the erection of hangars and derricks, the building of slipways and docks and the transportation of equipment such as tractors, coal, foodstuffs, clothing, gasoline and oil and all the other myriads of necessities … necessary for life in the Arctic. To transport all these things to a comparatively unknown region, select bases, erect buildings and enable the ships to leave before ice-fields barred their exit to the open sea … had no precedent.

The selection of suitable aircraft was a difficult one … (it) must be versatile and capable of operating off wheels, floats and skis and in addition must be extremely rugged in construction with if possible a cabin fuselage for protection against the severe cold and fitted with an absolutely reliable engine capable of operating under the most severe sub-zero conditions. In 1927, such an aircraft simply did not exist.

It was thus providential that in 1926 Anthony Fokker, the designer and builder of Germany's most famous fighters of WWI, had set up shop in New Jersey, USA. Along with his chief designer, Bob Noorduyn (of the Noorduyn 'Norseman'), Fokker … agreed to design and construct six aircraft to the desired specifications and within the prescribed three-month period. The product of their joint effort was the Fokker 'Universal' fitted with the Wright 225 HP radial, air-cooled 9-cylinder engine. The six aircraft were designed, built and delivered in exactly three months.

Personnel for the mission were selected; the RCAF provided six pilots and twelve airmen to fly and service the aircraft (including Flying Officer A. Lewis), the Army supplied one officer and three soldiers to build and maintain the wireless equipment, and the RCMP allotted one constable to each station. The civilian component was made up of nineteen persons including three medical doctors, three storekeepers and three cooks. The total complement for the three stations was forty-four souls.

July 1927 - at Halifax - leaving for Hudson's Straits.

L-R: F/L A.A. Leitch, F/O A.J. Ashton, F/L F.S. Coghill, S/C A. Lawrence, F/O B.G. Carr Harris, F/O A. Lewis

Two ships were selected: the ice-breaker CGS *Stanley* for the personnel, and a freighter SS *Larch* for the aircraft, stores, lumber, and construction crew of fifty-seven men. The expedition set sail from Halifax on July 15, 1927, and reached the Strait the beginning of August. By the end of October, the three bases had been established and the buildings erected after which the ships and carpenters sailed away for Halifax, narrowly missing being frozen in for the winter. An interesting feature in connection with the search for suitable bases was the incalculable value of a small Cirrus 'Moth' aeroplane on floats, which was carried on the after deck of the *Stanley* …. (W)hen required (it) could easily be lowered to the sea and flown inland up the innumerable inlets providing invaluable reconnaissance of the coastline … which by any other means … would have taken days and perhaps weeks.

Port Burwell, Hudson's Straits, 1927-28.

Life in the North

PORT BURWELL, DESIGNATED Base A, a former Moravian Mission site, was situated at the most northerly tip of Labrador, at the most easterly outlet of the Strait. The Eskimo[3] name, Killiniq, translated 'to the end of the earth' and seemed an apt description. The terrain was bare wind-swept rocks and towering cliffs with no vegetation of any kind, all frequently shrouded in cold mist or fog. It is here that Flying Officer Lewis was stationed. Nottingham Island at the western end of the Strait, designated Base B, was next set up, followed by Base C, Wakeham Bay[4], in the centre. All three bases were built and operational by the beginning of November, when both ships departed.

Alexander Lewis wrote:

The staple food at Port Burwell … is seal and next to seal, fish and next to fish, walrus. Seal is definitely an acquired taste; at first it tastes unbearably fishy … but eventually it becomes quite palatable. Seal liver is quite a delicacy … and is simply delicious fried with bacon. To the Eskimo, seal is manna from heaven; it provides him with practically everything he needs: food, clothing, boots and covering for his igloos during the summer thaw.

To kill a seal, the uninitiated will shoot as soon as the seal pokes its head above water; the Eskimo, on the other hand, will calmly wait for a few seconds and then fire. The reason for this is simple: if it is shot immediately it will sink but if permitted to fill its lungs with air and then shot it will remain afloat sufficiently long to enable the hunter to paddle alongside him and lift him aboard the kayak.

Walrus, although fishy, is much more palatable to eat than seal and not unlike beef in flavour; walrus meat is rich in protein and vitamins and … is invaluable for making up into such useful things as harness for the dog teams, thongs for whips and straps for lacing together the wood for

---

3   Though now considered offensive, Eskimo and Esquimo were terms used at the time, for the Inuit.

4   Now named Kangiqsujuaq [the large bay] in Inuktitut.

the *komatiks*. The ivory from the tusks is fashioned into harpoons, needles, fishing hooks and all such useful things normally made of iron and steel.

Polar bear when young are excellent as fresh meat but fishy and comparatively tender, the older polar bears however are extremely tough and good only for boiling down to blubber. Polar bear hide is much sought after and valuable in Eskimo terms of barter.

The fish is probably the best in the world. Arctic cod from ice-cold water literally melts in the mouth when cooked and the salmon-trout from the inland lakes in the wintertime would fetch fabulous prices in New York City. Fishing is simple in the Arctic; during the short summer the water is lucid clear and still ice-cold with the fish still unsophisticated in the wiles of man. All one has to do is to drop a line with two or three unbaited barbs secured to it and then wait for the rush. Cod will appear from all angles and dive for the hooks; the water being absolutely clear it is simple to watch for the psychological moment and pull cod up three at a time.

Bleak and lonely the Arctic may be but life there has its compensations. There are no financial problems for the simple reason that money simply doesn't exist, unlimited food for the catching, clothes for the hunting, snow-houses for the building, no morals between the sexes, yet no immorality, for the true nomad Eskimo is concerned only with the present and his immediate desires … In his natural, nomadic environment there is no better human living. He is sublimely unsophisticated, generous to a fault to the extent that he will share anything he possesses, including his woman, with anyone who is without. After a hunting expedition, his first action is to share his spoil with the rest of the village. A visitor likewise is treated handsomely; he is feasted and decked out with fresh clothing or his worn clothing mended, his sealskin boots or mukluks are chewed soft by the women and when he is ready to sleep he is provided with an Eskimo woman to keep him company through the long Arctic night. On the morning, he is supplied with fresh dogs to speed him on his way.

The Eskimo woman is a magnificent seamstress and a born boot chewer. She is responsible for the manufacture of all clothing including the magnificent parkas of caribou, polar bear and sealskin and also the completely waterproof sealskin boots. Her sewing of the boots is a masterpiece of craftsmanship; with her ivory needle she penetrates into only half the thickness of the skin and creates a perfect waterproof joint, unequalled by any professional boot factory.

After a day's hunting, sealskin boots become hard and stiff and uncomfortable on the feet. This is rectified by the women who, when the men return home, take their boots and for the rest of the night … chew them until the natural oils of the skins reassert themselves and render the boots soft and pliable. As a result of this perpetual chewing, an Eskimo woman's teeth are worn down flush with the gums.

The male Eskimo … is a marvelous imitator; if he is shown anything once he will copy it exactly without a flaw. He has a marvelous sense of humour and will roar with laughter at the simplest joke. He attains amazing skill at practical handicraft, yet seldom becomes sophisticated or cynical … He loves tobacco and is seldom seen without a pipe in his mouth, the women included, and smokes the strongest concoction he can get hold of, which is usually chewing tobacco soaked in molasses and rum.

The average Eskimo is a little man not much over four feet, but strong and sturdy with a thick layer of fat all over his body. He never washes but plasters himself with blubber fat and oil to keep the cold out and the heat in. The first impression one gets of an Eskimo is registered by the sense of smell. At first he appears to smell like a pole-cat and the women in particular, but as the months go by one becomes more accustomed to their particular odour and after a time they appear to smell quite normal. The women become quite good looking although at first they are really quite hard to take.

Such were our neighbours around Port Burwell, Wakeham Bay and Nottingham Island during the year 1927. This was an epic year for the Eskimo, for that was the first time … that the aeroplane was introduced to them. The aeroplane did not surprise them unduly much to our astonishment; apparently the reason for this was that they had always taken it for granted that the white man could achieve anything. On the other hand, they have such a high regard for their own ingenuity that they firmly believed that if they had access to the same resources and facilities as the white man, they also could do likewise.

The Eskimos took to flying as they did to their kayaks and *komatiks* and were not in the least disturbed when they left Mother Earth. Their ideas of geography were altered somewhat for they were able to see with their own eyes that instead of living on the end of the earth, there were other lands on the other side of the water. Frequent flights were made to Baffin Island … and at least one Eskimo was always taken along to give expert assistance in the building of igloos in the event of a forced landing. Likewise, the Eskimos of Baffin Island were similarly apprised of the fact that other lands existed and that other humans existed on them.

The Lewis Letters 47

Hudson's Straits 1927-8.

48   Pam McKenzie

Eskimo alphabet

a .b.d.e.g.i.j.k.l .m.n.o.p.r.s .t.u.v .y.

Oke su-ni,	(word of greeting which means : be strong.)
Ta-bou-e-tay,	(word of farewell)
Tik-i-pok,	the verb: to come. He, she, or it has come.
Tik-i-pOOnga	I have come
Tik-i-poogok	We two have come
Tik-i-pOO-goot	We all have come.
Kivok	It is coming also He or She.
Kivoonga	I am coming
Kivoogok	We two are coming
Kivoogoot	We all are coming
Kilai	Let it come, or bring it
O-ma-yak	Boat
Oo-woom-mut	To me.
Omayak kilai cowoom mut,	Bring the boat to me.
King-mik	Dog
King-mi-ga	My dog
Pia-me-vok	He, She or It wants
Pia-me-voonga	I want
Kingmik piamevoonga:	I want a dog.
Oowoonga piamevet	Do you want me
Mana	Now
Ma-nee	Here
Taba mana	Enough for now .

POO-LAK. TO VISIT.

Flying Operations

THE AIM OF the Hudson Strait Expedition was to fly daily patrols from each base to collect data on meteorological and ice conditions. Bad weather, however, regularly restricted flying; hills were obscured for days at a time and dense fog would roll in an average of one day in three. Still, from the end of September 1927 till mid-August 1928, the three bases flew 227 patrols for a total of 370 hours and took 2,285 photographs.

Port Burwell suffered the worst weather conditions of the three bases and also faced the additional challenge of operating in an area surrounded by cliffs. As it was not possible to build a hangar near the shore, one was constructed at the top of a cliff; a derrick was erected to raise and lower the aircraft onto a slipway when operating on floats, or to the ice when operating on skis. The base tractor figured prominently in this plan. It was first necessary to tow the aircraft out of the hangar to the derrick, lower both the tractor and the aircraft to the ice, then tow the aircraft over the rough shore ice to smoother ice farther out in the bay. As the ice conditions changed constantly due to wind and tide (a massive 22-foot rise and fall), it was necessary to re-select and prepare a strip of ice for each takeoff and landing.

In these severe weather conditions, the operation of both the tractor and aircraft engines was critical. Starting the tractor was a 20–30-minute endeavour using three or four blowtorches. The aircraft engine was similarly heated 30–40 minutes with blowtorches until the prop could be turned by hand. Warmed oil was then put in the tank and the engine revved to circulate the oil through the engine. This process was reversed at the end of a flight. While the engine was still running the oil would be drained, otherwise it would freeze before running out, adding extra hours of work with the thawing-out process.

Air navigation was similarly challenged. Although directional gyros had been invented, they were not in general use and not fitted in the Fokker aircraft. The magnetic compass proved to be grossly inaccurate due to the proximity of the Magnetic Pole and the presence of large deposits of magnetic ore in the rock formations. A magnetic variation of 54 degrees westerly was reported. Navigation was thus done by map-reading with maps largely inaccurate in detail but fairly reliable in salient features.

Each aircraft also carried a wireless transmitter, with a range of a hundred miles for voice and five hundred miles for key transmissions. This permitted an aircraft to communicate with its base but not receive a message in return. In cold weather, the pilots preferred the wireless key to voice due to the difficulty of handling a microphone while wearing face masks and heavy mitts. The airborne wireless equipment proved highly reliable through the length of the expedition.

52   Pam McKenzie

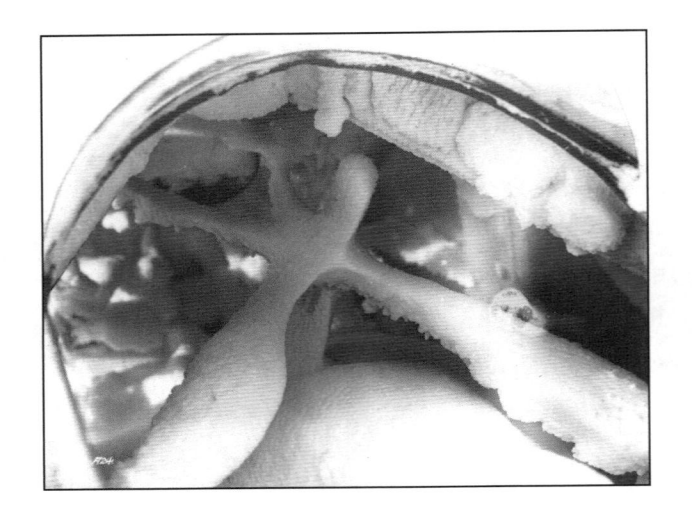

The Lewis Letters 53

Pam McKenzie

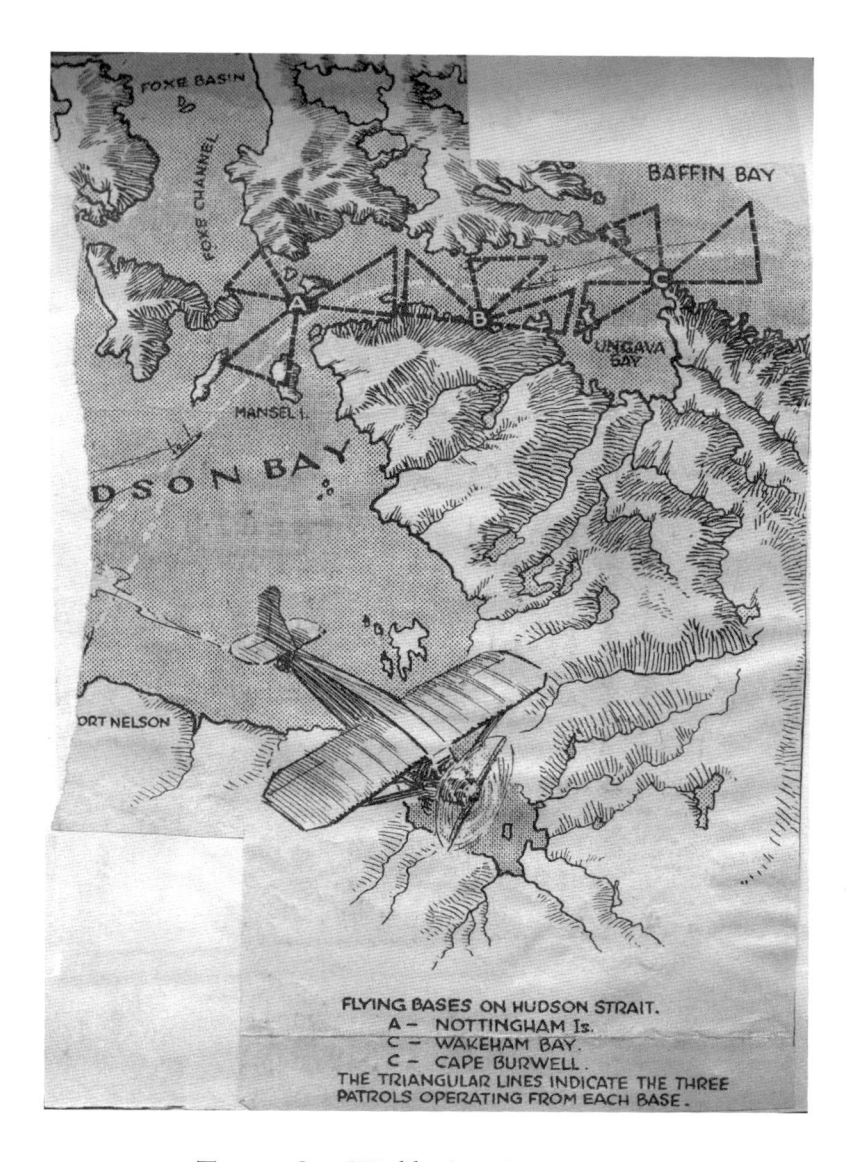

Toronto Star Weekly, Sat. Dec 31, 1927

Note to the Reader: The following is exactly as written by Alexander Lewis, edited for length, spelling and punctuation. Current in the northern vocabulary: a lead is an open area of water, a pan is a free-floating portion of ice and a *komatik* is a dog sled.

A Forced Landing on the Ice Floes

FRIDAY THE 17TH, 1928 to Thursday the 1st March, 1928, in which period Terry, Bobby and I came as near to death as ever we will be.

On the 17th of February 1928 at approximately 11 o'clock in the morning, I departed from Port Burwell on a regular ice patrol piloting Fokker aircraft G-CAHG with Flight Sergeant N. C. Terry as Engineer and an Esquimo named 'Bobby' Anakatok. He incidentally had only one eye and was known as 'Bobby the one-eyed Esquimo'. An Esquimo was carried on each flight to assist in building igloos in the event of a forced landing.

Our emergency equipment consisted of a rubber life-raft complete with CO_2 bottle, hand-pump and two paddles, a .303 high-powered rifle with fifty rounds of ammunition, a quantity of hard tack biscuits, some slabs of Baker's chocolate, several bottles of Horlick's Malted Milk tablets, a tin of butter, a tin of matches with soldered lid, two pounds of tea, a snow-knife for building igloos, three jackknives, fishing line and hooks, Primus stove and a gallon can of kerosene with a sealed screw-cap on the spout and three sleeping bags. The above list comprised the items we carried and used after our forced landing when making our way back to civilization.

Our route that day was direct across the Hudson Strait to Resolution Island, half-way up Frobisher Bay, returning across Grinnell Glacier and the Strait, back to the base. There were no weather forecasting facilities in those days so that each flight was always a bit of a gamble so far as the weather was concerned.

The weather and visibility on the outward trip were reasonably good but rapidly deteriorated on the homeward trip to the extent that having reached the Strait we ran into heavy snow of blizzard and hurricane proportions. I was forced to let down to within a few feet of the ice-pack where accurate navigation became well-nigh impossible what with the local magnetic disturbances, the oscillations of the compass needle, the extreme turbulence of the air and almost zero visibility. My chief problem was to keep right side up by visual mean, for there was no such aid as a directional gyro or turn-and-bank indicator.

It was obvious that it would have been next to miraculous for us to have reached our base under these conditions and in any event by this time our fuel was almost exhausted and barely enough to have reached home under ideal conditions. It was imperative that a decision be made immediately for total darkness was rapidly approaching and there were only two alternatives open to us: either to run out of fuel and then attempt a landing without an engine or to find a reasonably level stretch of ice and use our last drop of fuel by making a power-on landing. The hurricane was of such proportions that landing into it there should be practically no run after touching down practically eliminating any danger of a head-on collision into any of the numerous ice pinnacles.

The aircraft was fitted with a radio transmitter, so using the key I tapped out a message to base informing them that I was lost and was about to effect a landing on the ice-pack and that I was unaware of my exact location having been thrown considerably off course by the storm. Having sent the message, I held the aircraft dead into the wind and proceeded to look out for a suitable place to land. That was easier said than done for the ice pinnacles rose up out of the pack up to one hundred feet high, like a pincushion. At times we were down so low that I was obligated to dodge pinnacles seemingly appearing out of nowhere and the visibility was so poor that it was impossible to climb over them.

Terry, back in the cabin, told me afterwards that to him it was a veritable nightmare watching tall pinnacles of ice rushing past the windows of the aircraft at terrific speed, expecting each moment to be his last. Suddenly, I saw immediately below what appeared to be a stretch of clear, greenish ice and fervently praying that it extended ahead at least a short distance, I cut the engine. The aircraft dropped like a stone almost vertically and then using the engine for a short burst, I set it down on the ice and immediately cut the switches. When we hit the ice, so strong was the wind that the aircraft stopped almost immediately but the pinnacles were so numerous that we could not avoid hitting one head on. The aircraft finished up with the tail up in the air and the nose and skis buried in a deep snowdrift against an ice pinnacle.

I was thrown half out of the cockpit and it was an easy jump on to the ice. At the same time, Terry and 'Bobby' the one-eyed Esquimo, appeared out of the cabin door. When we looked around at what we had landed in, it seemed a miracle that we were not all killed. It was obvious that only the speed of the hurricane had saved us.

So far, so good. We were down safely with no bones broken. It was now almost quite dark and the immediate job was to build an igloo as quickly as possible if we were to keep from freezing to death. It was deathly cold and the wind seemed to blow right through us, so out came the emergency equipment from which we retrieved the snow-knife.

The first problem in building an igloo is to find a drift of snow sufficiently deep, from 10–15 feet is best, in order that one can dig down and build up at the same time. When a slab of snow is cut out of the drift it is placed on the edge of the hole; by working on the inside, only half the work is necessary and one can almost immediately start forming the domed roof.

The block of snow is cut out in the form of an arc of a circle. The builder on the inside continues to cut out these arcs until a complete circle is formed, placing each block on the outside edge of the hole. The top of each block is chamfered towards the centre with the result that they eventually meet in the form of a dome. The builder is at the same time digging down and when he has the igloo completed he leaves a block out for the remainder to crawl in then fills up the hole. While he has been building on the inside, the others have been stopping up the crevices between the blocks on the outside. When everyone is nicely tucked inside, a small hole for ventilation is cut out of the top of the dome. After a short time, the combined heat from the bodies within creates a thin coating of ice on the inner surface of the igloo making it completely windproof against the strongest winds.

We used the drift in which the aircraft had finished up and three of us working fast were able to complete our first igloo in about half an hour. Our sleeping bags and other emergency equipment were taken out of the aircraft and we proceeded to make ourselves comfortable. The first thing was to make some hot tea; getting out the Primus stove and filling it with kerosene, we soon had it roaring. Scraping off some snow from the inside of the igloo we melted it in a can and soon had some boiling water into which we threw a handful of tea. We had no sugar or milk but it tasted like nectar straight from the gods.

It was a great temptation to keep the Primus burning for it imparted to the little igloo a great feeling of comfort but it is most essential to extinguish any source of heat as soon as possible. If this is not done, a gentle rain will fall as the inner surface of the igloo melts. We decided not to consume any of our emergency rations for we had had breakfast before taking off and from now on we would eat only when it was absolutely necessary to maintain our strength. We decided however, to take an inventory of our rations and organize a method of rationing for the future. To do this it was first necessary to determine the maximum length of time the rations would have to last, and with that as a basis, decide on an absolute minimum ration necessary to maintain life.

In the first place, we were not exactly sure where we were, except that we were out at sea and not on land. Port Burwell forms the apex of a triangle with one of it sides the Labrador coast and the other the eastern coast of Ungava Bay. I had no idea which side of the apex of the triangle I was on: in the Atlantic Ocean or in Ungava Bay. After much consultation we came to the conclusion that if we did not reach safety in fifteen days, the rations wouldn't be of much use anyway. Our survival after that length of time in the middle of an Arctic winter out in the open would be highly problematical. We then proceeded to divide up the six slabs of chocolate, the hard tack biscuits and the Horlick Malted Milk tablets with mathematical precision. First of all into three equal parts, then each part into fifteen equal parts representing fifteen days' rations. I being the senior of the three made myself the custodian and distributor and stowed them away as part of the load I would have to carry. There appeared to be much more tea than we were likely to consume in fifteen days and the kerosene, if used sparingly, should also outlast that period. In addition, if we were lucky, we might come across some living thing to shoot … a seal, walrus or polar bear.

The Primus being now extinguished and the tea consumed, there was little else to do but climb into our sleeping bags and work out our future plan of action. Which direction to walk, east or west, it was a toss-up. If we were in the Atlantic then by walking east we would arrive nowhere, on the other hand, by walking west we would eventually reach the Labrador coast. If we were in Ungava Bay then by walking either east or west we would strike shore. In reconstructing the flight in my mind over and over again, I came to the conclusion that we must be in Ungava Bay. On the morrow, we would walk east towards Labrador. With that decision settled, I tried to sleep but with no success. Terry was in the same boat and must have been apprehensive as to the outcome of our adventure but he certainly didn't show it. With no outward sign of fear he remarked that he trusted my judgement implicitly. He was that kind of man, a perfect NCO with an inborn discipline born of a lifetime in the Service. It would never have entered his head to question any order, regardless of the danger.

We were both Englishmen, he a Cockney and I a Bristolian and proud of my heritage for being born in the city from which Sebastian and John Cabot sailed to discover the New World. As I pondered our critical situation, I wondered what John Cabot would have done under like circumstance. It passed through my mind that he must have survived much more fearful odds than lay before us and this thought gave me much cheer and courage.

When we had rested a few hours and collected our thoughts, we dug out of the igloo and finalized our plan of action before setting out on our first epic walk. The first thing to decide was the weight of equipment we each were physically able to carry. This is where Bobby came into the picture; he was a husky fellow, healthy and accustomed all his life to carrying big loads. He could carry at least half as much again as either one of us without any fatigue whatsoever. In addition, he could do with that one eye more than most people can do with two. He was a crack shot and seldom failed to bring down his quarry with the first shot; with only fifty rounds of ammunition at our disposal, Bobby was going to be worth his weight in gold.

It is a fallacy that Esquimos have an instinct of being able to find their way home by some sixth sense. On the other hand, they have an uncanny memory and will recognize landmarks at a glance and set off in the right direction without hesitation. Their ability to subsist off the country, their phenomenal stamina and resistance to fatigue and severe cold is the result of a lifetime of hunting and running alongside dog teams and consuming fabulous quantities of raw walrus, seal, fish and polar bear. An Esquimo generates a tremendous amount of heat and even under the most severe conditions his hands will always be warm even without any covering.

The clothing of the average Esquimo usually consists of a Hudson Bay Co. parka made from a kind of woolen Duffel, a wind-break parka of sealskin or caribou skin on the outside, woolen Duffel socks, sealskin waterproof boots and Mackinaw trousers. Their gloves usually consist of unborn seal next to the skin with ordinary sealskin on the outside. For our part we were clad in chamois leather underclothing for flying, Duffel shirts and pullovers, Duffel socks in shoe packs, flying helmets and a light eiderdown flying suit, very fine in texture and very light in weight. Our gloves were the same as worn by the Esquimo.

We were therefore all adequately clothed, perhaps over-clothed for continuous walking. We resolved that if it proved to be too much we would discard articles of clothing en route until we had reached the comfortable minimum. Our next problem was to decide what we intended to carry with us and what we were going to leave with the aircraft. The first important item were the rations, next the sleeping bags, the rubber life raft and paddles, the rifle and fifty rounds of ammunition, the compass dismantled from the aircraft, the eight-day clock, and the smaller items such as clasp knives, fishing line and hooks, snow-knife, matches, etc.

Bobby was made the custodian of the life raft, paddles and snow-knife. The primus stove and kerosene became Terry's charge; we each carried our own sleeping bag. I became the custodian of the rations, compass, clock and smaller items. Bobby insisted on carrying the rifle and ammunition for to an Esquimo a rifle is as valuable as life itself. This division of load took some time and half the short period of daylight was already gone, so without further ado and gravely saluting the aircraft adieu, we set out on our journey. It is a sad experience to take leave of an aircraft under such conditions. When airborne over barren wastes, an aircraft conveys a sense of great security; a false security perhaps when engines were not as reliable as they are today. A false security which is poignantly brought home when one is forced to land.

The blizzard of the day before had now been replaced by a strong northwest gale, with overcast skies, poor visibility and a very low temperature. When walking under such conditions one normally walks from fatigue to fatigue, but we would have to disregard fatigue and walk from first light to last light. Esquimos when on the move travel from sleep to sleep and do not bother about night and day; they speak of a place being so many sleeps away. The more hardy Esquimo will have fewer sleeps between places than the normal run and take a pride in completing a journey in as few sleeps as possible.

We could have only walked about two hours that first day, yet one thing about the condition of the ice gave me grounds for considerable thought. I had anticipated that walking towards a shore, the ice conditions should improve gradually to the extent that the pinnacles should become smaller and the floes less rough for walking. And yet the reverse was the case: the pinnacles were becoming taller and the floes rougher to the extent that they were rapidly becoming almost impossible to negotiate. The visibility was too poor for any possibility of sighting land, so no help could be expected from that direction. I decided to call a halt at once, build an igloo and reserve our energies until I had thought out this new situation in the comparative comfort of our igloo and sleeping bags.

We soon found a drift of snow sufficiently deep which we could build our igloo and in less than half an hour were comfortably ensconced within, drinking tea and consuming our meagre ration. I disclosed my fears to Terry. I told him that my original estimation of our position was probably in error and that we were in fact in the Atlantic Ocean. By walking east we were walking out to sea.

He replied very simply that all we had to do then, was to walk in the opposite direction. Walking towards the west must eventually bring us to a shore irrespective of whether we were in the Atlantic or Ungava Bay, so we decided to play it safe and on the morrow, reverse our steps to the west.

We were now somewhat easier in our minds and looked forward to the morrow with some degree of excitement, with the added hope that the visibility may be good enough for us to catch some glimpse of land. If we were really in the Atlantic, we could not possibly be beyond the range of vision of the Labrador mountains. They are at least two to three thousand feet high with snow-covered peaks, which should stand out vividly in the sky. I prayed for a clear day on the morrow, which would confirm my calculations of our position.

We were very tired and did not awake until the light was well advanced. Digging our way out of the igloo we discovered a beautiful, clear, exceedingly cold day, so cold that the air was alive with electricity. Every movement we made was reflected by crackling sounds in the atmosphere. We were completely surrounded by tightly packed ice pinnacles and could not immediately sight anything on the horizon. Climbing to the top of one, I was almost afraid to look towards the west for if I saw nothing it would dash all our hopes for survival. When I at last glanced to the west, there clearly etched in the sky, were mountain peaks white with snow. I could scarcely contain my joy. A rough calculation convinced me that we must be about fifty miles out in the Atlantic. Taking into consideration the height of the mountains, in an aeroplane at three thousand feet on a clear day, one has a range of vision of approximately fifty miles. A further proof should be apparent as we progressed towards the shore by the progressive improvement of the ice floes for walking, and the diminution and spreading out of the pinnacles.

With renewed hope and enthusiasm, we reversed all our previous ideas and commenced to retrace our steps in a westerly direction. Terry and I both realized that there would be no turning back a second time and our lives were now at stake. With this poignant thought in mind we turned our backs on the east and our footsteps to the west.

Halifax Herald, Feb. 20, 1928

STILL HOPING TO FIND MISSING AIRMEN ALIVE

Commander of Hudson Strait Expedition Says Situation Uncertain, However

(Canadian Press Despatch.)

Ottawa, Feb. 22.—"We have by no means given up hope that they will be found alive," declared Major N. B. McLean, of the department of marine and commander of the Hudson Straits expedition, in reference today to the fate of the two aviators and the Eskimo who have been lost for nearly a week somewhere in the ice fields of the Arctic wastes 4 hours and 25 minutes of flying time from Port Burwell, their base.

"We admit that the situation is very ticklish and uncertain," Major McLean said, "but we feel that we may have hope for a long time yet. Even should the plane have gone off its course out over the North Atlantic we feel that it may have come down on the moving ice and might drift ashore along the Labrador coast, where the men would be pretty certain to reach some sort of settlement."

HOPE WANES FOR MISSING FLIERS; BELIEVED DEAD

Planes Comb Hudson Straits But Fail to Find Trace of Lost Airmen

COMRADES BRAVE COLD AND STORMS IN HUNT

Provisions Must Be Exhausted —Last Word From Them February 17

Tuesday planes from the three bases at Burwell, Wakeham Bay and Nottingham Island combed Ungava Bay, as far south as Leaf Bay, but no trace of the missing men could be found. Whether they were blown out into the open Atlantic in the blizzard which forced them to descend, or whether they may have landed near the coasts of Baffin Island can not be determined. The last communication from them was last Friday, when they wirelessed their base that they were lost and were trying to make a landing. Since then there has been no word of them. This, coupled with the fact that they can communicate by wireless only when their plane is in the air, would seem to indicate that they had not again taken off.

Their comrades are fulfilling all the best traditions of the Royal Canadian air force in braving the storms and extreme cold of these latitudes in an effort to locate the missing men.

ABANDON HOPE FOR AIRMEN

Government Officials' Fear Aviators Lost in North Are Dead

SEARCH CONTINUES

(Canadian Press Despatch)

Ottawa, Ont., Feb. 22—At noon today no news had been received from the air stations on the Hudson Straits with regard to the fate of the two airmen, Flying Officer Lewis and Flying Serg. Terry, and the native who accompanied them on their flight last Thursday.

Little hope was held out by government officials here that the men missing from the air base at Port Burwell, in the Hudson Straits, since Feb. 17, are still alive. The party carried three days' rations with them, and these must have become exhausted long ago. At the same time, it seemed altogether impossible that they could have survived the exposure for any length of time.

...fully equipped, it is trusted that Officer Lewis and his companions will survive the elements until either the searching 'planes or the dog-sled party come upon them.

OTTAWA, Feb. 22—Little hope was held out by government officials here that the two airmen, Flying Officer Lewis and Flight Sergeant Terry, and the native, who have been missing from the air base at Port Burwell, in the Hudson Straits, since February 17, still are alive.

The party carried three days' rations with them, and these must have become exhausted long ago. At the same time, it seemed impossible that they could have survived the exposure for any length of time.

Yesterday planes from the three bases at Burwell, Wakeham Bay and Nottingham Island combed Ungava Bay, as far south as Leaf Bay, but no trace of the missing men could be found.

Fate Unknown

Whether they were blown out into the open Atlantic in the blizzard which forced them to descend,

Flying Officer A. Lewis

Toronto Daily Star, Feb. 24, 1928

During the first hour or so, there appeared to be little change in the formation of the ice pack. The going was slow and arduous; at times we were up to our waists in snow, at others walking on perfectly clear, greenish sponge ice. The ice gave to our weight as we walked on it and emitted a weird squeezing sound. Again we were forcing our way through tightly packed ice pinnacles, jammed together by a fierce storm. Occasionally, we were forced to scale such jams to maintain our compass course and eliminate extra miles of walking in order to circumvent them. It was shortly after scaling one such formation that I detected a change for the better. Both Terry and I were convinced that the pinnacles ahead were smaller and not so tightly packed, to the extent that we could see through them. From now on it would be possible to walk directly on the compass.

We were so completely satisfied that we were on the right track and as the light was rapidly diminishing, we decided to call a halt at the first good drift and turn in for the night. Our renewed confidence was reflected in our increased cheerfulness; we built our igloo with gusto, singing as we worked. This one only took us seventeen minutes to complete; from now on, we decided, this time should be the standard to work to at the end of each day's trek. And so ended the second day with far different feelings than the day before when we had felt that we had reached our slough of despond.

During the night in the igloo musing over our situation, I felt that although many hardships lay ahead, there was a sporting chance that we would survive. I had visions of striking shore, slowly wending our weary way over mountains, through valleys and along the coast, living off the country by fishing and shooting and eventually arriving back at the base resplendent with beards and fat as Esquimos. Beards were already becoming a reality and a nuisance because of the large blobs of ice that would form on them by the freezing of our breath as we walked.

Our tummies were now beginning to feel the strain of insufficient food in proportion to the consistent, unaccustomed exercise. It would be necessary before long to obtain some kind of fresh meat. We were, after all, walking all day long over abnormally rough terrain with nothing more to eat than a small piece of hard tack biscuit and a still smaller piece of chocolate. There is no nourishment in tea, although it certainly provides wonderful mental relaxation and is a mild form of narcotic.

The greatest hardship of all was the complete absence of fresh water. It is a fallacy that all one has to do is to chop off a piece of ice floe and suck it; nothing is farther for the truth. When floes and pinnacles are being formed, salt is precipitated and forms a thick crust on the outside. Even snow in contact with ice becomes tainted as we discovered to our disgust. The only way to obtain fresh snow is to scoop it from the centre of a pile and then melt it in the mouth. I know of nothing in the world less satisfying than a mouthful of snow when one is parched with thirst. It is as if one had swallowed a mouthful of sand. At the end of each day's march, our first action was to melt snow over the Primus and drink our fill. We would have given almost anything for a drink of cool, clear water on the march.

On the following day when we cut our way out of the igloo, the temperature was comparatively mild but it was snowing heavily with a strong wind from the east and practically no visibility. We would have to plod on monotonously on our compass course with no sight of our mountains, taking comfort in the gradually improving ice conditions. Chances were, with poor visibility, another day would pass without sighting anything to kill.

We must have been walking for three or four hours when suddenly we came on to open water. It was a lead, about twenty yards wide and an indeterminate length due to poor visibility. This is where the life raft was going to get its christening and we our maiden voyage. Off came the raft from Bobby's back, out came the hand pump, the paddles we had been using for walking. We soon had it well pumped up and proceeded to launch. It was fortunate the wind was in our favour but it looked too frail to carry the three of us at once. We decided to make two trips with Bobby as the pilot, given his lifetime experience of kayaks. Bobby was in his element, compared to a frail kayak which is merely a sealskin shell, the raft to him was a luxury craft. The fact that it was round made it extremely difficult to navigate in a straight line, but Bobby soon overcame its vagaries and in short order had us safely across on the other side.

The storm was abating somewhat but the light was rapidly declining. Crossing the lead had consumed much valuable time and there was little left to us for finding a suitable drift for an igloo. The level of the floe did not lend itself to the formation of deep drifts and it appeared we would have to spend a long, cold, weary night out in the open. The snow and wind had been replaced by a rapidly falling temperature and it looked as if we were in for a most uncomfortable night.

At this point I should refer to an interesting item of our emergency rations, which I have purposely omitted until now. An item for the safety of which I had made myself personally responsible:

a bottle of Hennessy's Three-Star Brandy. It passed through my mind that this was going to be one time when it would be really appreciated. Although I am virtually a teetotaler, the name of Hennessey's Three Star still sounds like music in mine ears, for on that night it tasted like nectar from the gods.

Darkness was now upon us, the only thing to do was find some sort of protection against the wind and huddle up together in our sleeping bags and keep as warm as we could. The very condition that augured so well for our survival, the smoother condition of the floes, would militate against us by denying sufficient shelter to sleep. We stopped at some low pinnacles jammed together and scraped together sufficient snow to form a low enclosure. In the lee of the pinnacles we got the Primus going and made some boiling hot tea. Sleep was out of the question for we were apprehensive as to whether we would ever awake if we were unable to keep sufficiently warm. It was then that I decided that this was a sufficient emergency to justify use of the brandy. Every so often when we felt the cold penetrating into the very marrow of our bones, Terry and I would take a sip and it seemed as if new life was flowing through us. Bobby wasn't interested; he had never tasted liquor and had always been warned by the missionaries that it was the devil liquid. We did not try to dissuade him. I am quite sure that had it not been for the boiling hot tea and the frequent sips of brandy, we would not have survived.

Terry and I had plenty of misgivings as to the outcome of this affair but we never, by even the slightest gesture or whisper, permitted Bobby to become aware of it. His knowledge of English was confined to about a dozen words; we conversed with him in his native tongue, a language we made it our business to master during the first few weeks of our arrival in the Arctic. Bobby was blissfully confident that we knew exactly where we were going and how long it would take us and that all he had to do was pad along with us in order to arrive back at our base in due time. Strangely enough, he never questioned our complete about turn after the first day, yet he must have realized that we were going in the opposite direction. As we lay there that night, I estimated we were covering ten miles a day so should reach shore in another three days, barring accidents; if anything the going should be getting progressively better. We decided that when the weather cleared we should be getting a full moon and then we would walk through the night and get off the floes as quickly as possible.

The night had been cold and clear and augured well for the day. We were anxiously awaiting broad daylight and good visibility to see our mountains again. We had only been walking half an hour when to our intense joy, the dark shadow of the mountains loomed right ahead of us. As the light improved, the peaks seemed to stretch up to the sky out of sight. We seemed to be only a short distance away from them, though this of course was an illusion. Bobby became almost hysterical and it was all we could do to restrain him from running towards them. Eventually we calmed him down and prevailed on him to conserve his strength for sterner things to come.

From now on during daylight hours, the compass was no longer necessary. There were two peaks taller than the rest and consulting our maps salvaged from the aircraft, I found a spot designated as 'Four Peaks', apparently eighty miles down the Labrador coast from Port Burwell. If the two we could see were part of this group, we had drifted a considerable distance south with the Labrador Current and would continue to do so while we remained on the floes. We should have allowed for drift by walking at an angle towards the shore, but we were so completely fed up with the ice pack that we decided to disregard drift and reach shore as quickly as possible. The Labrador coast was rapidly assuming the quality of a land flowing with milk and honey. We had visions of freshwater lakes teeming with fish, seals close to shore, polar bear, and an unlimited supply of snowdrifts for igloos. If we could only reach shore, our survival seemed assured.

On we walked in seemingly endless monotony in a temperature so cold and dry that our clothing cracked as we moved. Suddenly, to our utter astonishment, immediately ahead of us was a most extraordinary sight. It was a wide lead, perhaps sixty to seventy yards wide, and in it, diving and gamboling to their heart's content, were literally hundreds of walrus. The entire lead was teaming with them! This was the first sign of life we had come across since our forced landing and right before our eyes was more fresh meat than we could have imagined in our wildest dreams.

The catch was that we were not equipped for walrus hunting, for we had no harpoon. To shoot a walrus in the water is a sheer waste of ammunition for it will merely sink to the bottom. Our only chance of shooting one was to wait until we could see one on solid ice. We waited for at least a half hour when one huge fellow lumbered to the edge of the lead, dragged himself up onto the ice and commenced to roll. Bobby slowly cocked the rifle and with his one eye took steady aim and fired. The walrus leapt several feet in the air and almost fell back into the water again; when we got to him he was half on and half off the ice.

Immediately, Bobby proceeded to cut into the still living animal, for though the walrus was stunned by the shot in the head, he was still alive and breathing heavily. Bobby cut a huge slab of flesh out of his side and ravenously devoured it. Hungry as we were for fresh meat, Terry and I drew the line at eating living flesh and decided to wait until it was frozen when we could chop it into small squares and swallow them whole. While Bobby was gorging himself, we carved out as much meat as we thought we could carry and laid it out on the ice to freeze which it did rapidly in about fifteen minutes. We cut it into small squares and added them to our greatly depleted rations. This incident was probably the real turning point in our adventure for it had been obvious for some time that the rations were grossly inadequate for the amount of energy we were expending. We had visions of cooking some of our walrus when we reached shore if our kerosene lasted that long, but at the moment we intended to conserve our meagre supply for melting snow and making tea.

It took a little time to get organized again after all this excitement, but eventually we collected ourselves, unpacked the raft and prepared for our second voyage across the lead. We were obliged to walk at least a mile along the edge of the lead to select a spot where there were the least walruses. This time we decided to make one crossing with the three of us on board owing to the considerable width of the lead and the strong wind from the north. Strangely enough the extra weight gave it additional stability and made it easier to steer. So, giving the walruses a wide berth, it was not long before we were safely on the other side.

Leaving Bobby to pack up the raft, Terry and I consulted to decide whether to continue on the same course and reach shore as quickly as possible, or strike diagonally into the drift and cut off a few miles of coast. We decided again to continue on a straight course, and off we went with renewed vigour and optimism until dark, when we found an excellent drift at the base of a pinnacle and dug ourselves in for the night. We had our igloo completed in record time and the three of us were in high spirits, now supremely confident that it was merely a matter of time when we would be safely back at our base. Once comfortably settled, I made a routine check of our equipment and missed the familiar bulk of the life raft. I concluded that Bobby had forgotten to bring it in, but after some confusion and questioning, I elicited the fact that he had deliberately left it behind by the lead in order to carry its weight in walrus flesh. In his mind the reasoning was perfectly sound, provided that there were no more leads to cross. Unfortunately, I was convinced that as we neared the shore the leads would, if anything, become more numerous. Time was too precious to waste it in returning to look for it, so we decided philosophically not to cross our bridges until we came to them, in true Esquimo fashion, and slept our first real night's sleep in two nights.

Awakening the next day after a good seven hours sleep, we breakfasted on frozen walrus squares, biscuit, chocolate and two cups of tea each. Feeling like normal men again, we set out on our way, but not without a careful check of our inventory. The day was overcast, not quite so cold and the wind had veered to the east with a light snow falling. The visibility was not as good as the day before and the mountains could only just be made out ahead. We had only gone a short distance when we espied huge, fresh tracks in the snow, unmistakably polar bear. We were so keen on getting off the floes that we had no enthusiasm for tracking him; we had ample supply of fresh meat for the time being. We were fortunate that he had not discovered our igloo while we slept for he could have crushed it with one blow of a huge paw. This potential danger had not occurred to us and was another reason for reaching shore as soon as possible. His tracks were, however, a definite indication that we must be in the vicinity of seal and from now on we should have little worry about food.

The rest of the day passed uneventfully and we were fortunate in finding a nice drift before light gave out and passed the night without incident. The next day proved to be similar to the previous one: overcast, windy and comparatively mild, with poor visibility. The going was good, rough underfoot at times but with no tall ice to negotiate. At times, we would be walking for several miles on soft, green, sponge ice, which felt remarkably like walking on a soft green carpet. The coastline could now be clearly made out and appeared to be just a few miles away. In fact, with a bit of luck, I thought that we might make shore without any more sleeps on the ice floes.

We had been walking for about two hours when my worst fears were realized: there ahead of us lay a lead, not a very wide one, but still a lead that would have to be negotiated without a raft. Bobby was devastated! He realized that he had prejudiced our chances of survival and at the very least, prolonged our stay on the ice. It was impossible to determine how far the lead stretched in either direction to walk around it. There was nothing to do but walk north in the direction of the drift. At least our extra walking would not be a dead loss by counteracting the drift of the Labrador Current.

We had been walking for about an hour towards the north when we noticed that the ice on the edge of the lead was becoming ragged and cracked as if it would take very little prying to release a pan of it away from the main pack. We decided to watch for a suitable condition which would enable us to release a pan sufficiently large to support the weight of the three of us and use it as a raft to ferry us across to the other side.

Our progress slowed, but eventually we came across a condition which looked favourable. Striving with everything we possessed in the way of knives, paddles and our bare hands, we succeeded in separating a fairly nice pan from the main pack. The big question now was would it support the combined weights of the three of us? Bobby took a flying leap onto the centre of it and kept it level while we in turn jumped on. Under our combined weights, the pan sank into the water at least three inches; our feet were awash in ice-cold water and rapidly becoming numb. We crouched down as low as we could to prevent the pan from capsizing and quickly paddled our way across. When we hit shore, Terry in his hurry to get off, slipped and fell into the water. We quickly pulled him out; his immersion gave us some concern but the water had not penetrated his clothing sufficiently to cause him any great discomfort. Thanks to the fact that his clothing was made up of waterproof skins, he suffered no ill effects whatsoever. Our feet also, although numb with cold, were still dry thanks to the sealskin mukluks.

We congratulated ourselves on another crisis successfully averted but the light was nearly gone. Life on the floes had become a veritable nightmare and we determined that, come what may, our next sleep would be on shore. We would continue to plod on through the darkness. One thing in our favour was the considerable improvement in the surface of the ice and the fact that our compass was luminous. Our speed was of necessity slow, but at least the exercise kept us warm until we reached such a state of fatigue that we were obliged halt. We bivouacked in the lee of an ice ridge and there remained until dawn, drinking tea and sipping brandy. Fortunately, the cold was not intense during the night although the wind was blustery and whistled eerily over the ice. With our ever-increasing optimism, the hours passed quickly and we were up and on our way again at first light.

It was fortunate that we had decided to stop when we did, for the surface of the ice became extremely rough and continued to be so right up to the shore. I had been under the impression that all we had to do was to simply walk ashore but such was not the case. That particular part of the coastline was actually just about the worst spot to come ashore, as I noticed in succeeding days during our trek up the coast.

We literally raced onto the shore and up the cliff away from the hateful ice floes. As soon as we struck shore we fell down on our knees and kissed the rock. There was nothing else but bare rock and snow but at least it was land. Any storms from now on would be known factors at least and the ground was not likely to open up underneath us. Our first thought was to find a drift and build an igloo. We found a wonderful site half-way up the cliff, hidden from the floes. There was certainly not going to be any dearth of drifts from now on, for that winter there had been an unusually heavy fall of snow. Our main problem looked as if it might be contending with the deep snow on our trek over the mountains to the north.

Northwards up the Labrador Coast to Port Burwell

IT WAS STILL broad daylight when we had completed the building of our igloo; there was no great urgency to continue our journey now that we were off the floes. When we were comfortably settled inside our sleeping bags, drinking tea and eating our rations, we commenced drawing up our next plan of action. The first thing to do was determine our position on the coast. With the 'Four Peaks' as our datum point and taking into consideration the drift of the floes, we decided that we must be approximately ninety miles down the coast from Port Burwell. If that assumption were correct, then we should be somewhere between Nachvak and Nanuktok and by walking north for approximately twenty miles, we should strike the inlet of Kamaktorvik. If we were further south than we calculated, then by still walking north we should strike Nachvak where we knew there was an Esquimo settlement. I was confident in my own mind however, that we were north of Nachvak, but not so confident that I was willing to take a chance and walk south to reach it. Esquimos invariably live in close proximity to the coast, for their existence is solely dependent on seal, fish, driftwood and the fruit of the sea. In wintertime, they often trek inland to fish for salmon-trout through holes in the frozen inland lakes. By adhering fairly close to the coastal regions, there would be the chance that we would come across some Esquimo hunters either proceeding to or returning from their hunting or fishing grounds, or at least old *komatik* tracks, which we could follow to their place of origin.

When we awoke and dug ourselves out of the igloo, the day was already far advanced and the weather was clear and very cold with a strong northwest wind. Shouldering our belongings off we went, turning our steps for the first time towards the north. After having covered a few miles overland we realized that this next phase was not going to be any sinecure. The going was infinitely rougher than we had anticipated, with the snow many feet deep and at times up to our waists. We now regretted that we had not followed the coast. Looking back I now realize how foolish it was attempting to scale mountains and negotiate valleys, but the mind plays strange tricks with our judgement when the body is starved. Our decision had been entire a psychological one, the reaction to those horrible days and nights spent on the floes, which repelled us from the frozen sea and drove us inland. Rather than retrace our steps, we decided to plod on overland until we came across the first inlet and from then on adhere more rigidly to the coastline. After about ten miles of most arduous walking, we decided to call it a day, build an igloo, sleep and draw up another plan of action. We decided to scale the mountain we were now on and when at its highest point obtain a good view and a more accurate fix on our position.

The next day dawned very cold and clear and the North-Wester[5] had increased in strength. If I live to be a hundred I shall never forget climbing that mountain in the face of the northwest wind, through deep snow drifts, over dangerous crags and up a long steep glacier lying in a gully. We had decided that the glacier would be the easiest method of crossing the mountain. The gully in which it lay was protected from the main force of the wind, and the walking although slippery, was reasonably easy. That is until we arrived at a point abreast with the crest of the mountain and caught the full force of the North-Wester, which must have been of full-gale proportions. We were trying to climb up against it as best we could when I lost my balance, slipped and started to roll down the way we had just come.

Those first few terrible moments will never be forgotten: rolling over and over, down and down, with increasing momentum into eternity. Suddenly, I pulled up short and found myself buried in a deep drift. Climbing out and looking around, I beheld to my astonishment, Terry within a few yards of me. He had been swept off his feet in exactly the same way. But the can of kerosene he

---

5   Many would now call it a Nor'Wester.

had been carrying had been torn from his grasp and lay between two rocks a hundred feet below. If the can were broken and our precious kerosene lost, goodbye to our one and only comfort, hot boiling tea at the end of each day's labours. Terry was soon down after it, and when he retrieved it, he immediately put up his thumb signaling that everything was alright and no damage done.

Bobby, during all this, had retained his balance and was now making his way down to help us. We tried to stop him, but he was taking the easy way and sliding down on his bottom under perfect control. He seemed to be thoroughly enjoying it; he had obviously done this before and welcomed the opportunity of doing it again. The Esquimo takes an almost childish delight in executing stunts of this nature to work off his love for excitement. When he is out on the water in his kayak, he loves to thrill the ones on shore by doing a complete roll under the water and up the other side, grinning his head off.

When we had collected ourselves, we recommenced the ascent of the glacier. This time we determined to leave the glacier before we attempted to breast the crest and take full advantage of any protection that would present itself. We reached the crest amid drifts and rocks and gullies filled with snow so deep we sank almost out of sight, until complete and utter fatigue made it impossible to continue. We selected a site protected from the wind behind a crag and dug ourselves in for the night, completely worn out. We resolved henceforth never to attempt the scaling of mountains again and to adhere rigidly to the coast from now on.

The next day was overcast with milder temperatures and an east wind. It was not long before we had breasted the crest entirely and there ahead of us we beheld a great plateau. It was completely windswept and level as a billiard table, with a smooth surface of hard encrusted windswept snow. We must have been up very high for the slightest exertion made itself felt; this was probably the reason why we were so fatigued on the previous day. The frozen sea appeared to be at a great depth beneath us and it appeared as if there were an inlet or indentation in the mountains at the other side of the plateau. There was a definite line of demarcation between the plateau and the next mountain peak ahead.

When I look back on this incident I recall a most exhilarating feeling. Walking along that plateau high up in the sky, on a perfectly smooth surface of snow, was a feeling so pleasant that it dispelled all recollection of the hardships we had undergone. We were actually beginning to enjoy the adventure for the first time.

We had been walking thus for about two hours when we decided to call a halt, rest awhile and partake of a slight repast of raw walrus and snow. We then continued our pleasant stroll along the plateau until we reached the other extremity. Lo and behold, there lay beneath us a long wide inlet stretching out of sight into the mountains from the sea. This inlet appeared to be as smooth as the surface of our plateau and if so, our progress would now be considerably faster and easier. However, to reach this inlet there was first a steep mountainside to descend.

The first half of the descent proved to be as difficult as the latter half of the ascent, and our progress was extremely slow. It was impossible to find a route where there was any possibility of walking. All we could do was to jump from crag to crag, gingerly wade through deep drifts not knowing if we were about to be engulfed in one, and wend our way in a zigzag route to circumvent the steep chasms with which the mountainside abounded. When it appeared we had negotiated the halfway mark, we called a halt by a huge snowdrift, dug ourselves a veritable palace of an igloo, and there we remained until dawn.

When we consulted our maps in the igloo that night, it was clear that the inlet beneath us must be Kamaktorvik. Across the other side, approximately twenty-five or thirty miles away, was Eclipse Harbour, a large Esquimo settlement. Our supply of walrus meat was running perilously low and it would be vitally necessary to renew it in some form, another reason we should get down to the coastline again as soon as possible. Before long we fell into a sound sleep and did not awaken until the light was well advanced.

The next day was cold and clear with our old friend the North-Wester back in our faces. But this time we were going down the mountain instead of up, so our spirits were high and we went off with renewed vigour. The second half of the descent was remarkably easy to negotiate by comparison with the first. Although it was necessary to zigzag continuously, the drifts were becoming less deep and the descent less steep. Eventually, with a sigh of relief, we set foot on the inlet.

The surface of the inlet was as smooth and level as it had appeared from the top of the plateau. It was paved with a hard crust of windswept snow, slightly corrugated by the action of the wind. The largest aircraft could have landed and taken off, either on wheels or skis, in almost any direction. I judged the inlet to be about two miles across from where we stood; with excellent walking conditions, we should reach Eclipse Harbour in one or two sleeps at the most.

We set off in line abreast across the inlet, with Bobby on the left, Terry in the centre and I on the right. We had been walking for about an hour when Bobby let out a most terrific yell; startled, we dashed to his side. His one keen eye had picked out the familiar tracks of *komatik* runners. They were of fairly recent vintage, for they were not yet filled in by the action of the wind, and ran from one side of the inlet to the other. Terry turned to me and held out his hand, remarking simply 'I guess we're saved'. I shook hands with him and answered 'We certainly are.' It was an extraordinary ritual to take place in such a godforsaken place.

There was no way of determining in which direction the *komatik* had passed, but it was obvious that the settlement from which it came must be on the coast. All we had to do now was to follow the tracks towards the coast and on towards Eclipse Harbour, where I was confident the tracks had their origin. We set off this time in single file down the centre of the tracks, Bobby taking up the rear, Terry in the centre and I ahead. We continued in this fashion walking in absolute silence for at least two hours, each one of us lost in his thoughts. Suddenly I was startled out of my wits by a deafening yapping of dogs. Jumping around, I beheld almost at my heels, a dog team and *komatik* and three Esquimos, a man, a woman and a little boy. Bobby and Terry had been picked up a few minutes before and I, in sublime ignorance, was still plodding on, oblivious to our sudden good fortune.

Bobby was almost hysterical, jabbering away at top speed in his own particular dialect, explaining to our newfound friends exactly what had happened to us. As we surmised, they were from

Eclipse Harbour and had been on a fishing exhibition to an inland lake and were now returning home. They had spotted us early that morning, shortly after dawn, as we had set foot on the inlet. They thought at first that we must be caribou, for it was impossible for human beings to be in such a place without dogs or *komatik*. After a short time, particularly when the dogs caught the scent, nothing could stop them until they eventually caught up with us. If we had only glanced around just once during the day, all our troubles would have been over. Our minds had become almost hypnotized on the one important fact that we must continue on our course come what may. As it was, it took them the greater part of that day to catch us. It was a stroke of luck that they had chosen an inland lake from which they had a panorama of the entire inlet. Three objects walking stood out like the Sphinx in the Sahara.

The tracks we had discovered had of course been made by them on their outward trip. After the excitement had abated somewhat, they invited us over to their *komatik* and hauled out some beautiful salmon-trout, the result of their fishing trip. They hacked off some splinters with a small axe; the frozen fish melted in our mouths; seldom had anything tasted so good. We were still parched for a drink of fresh water and they informed us of a fine lake almost on our route, where fresh water would appear at a certain spot, under the snow. We could hardly believe it when we proceeded inland for about a mile, came across the frozen lake, and at the edge, under the snow, was beautiful spring water bubbling furiously underneath. It was like a dream when we were able to kneel down and drink our fill of such beautiful water. Brandy may be an excellent stimulant in times of emergency, but in my opinion there can be no better stimulant in the world than a drink of fresh, cold, spring water when one's resistance has reached its lowest ebb.

Mentally, I for one, seemed to be walking in a dream and to this day vividly recall the exultant feeling of our meeting with the Esquimos. Our bodies had suffered immeasurably through lack of adequate food and exposure to sub-zero cold; Terry's and my hands and face were badly frostbitten under our beards and most painful and sore. I had a strange feeling of lightheadedness about this period and was daily becoming less communicative, the logical effects of a starved body on a tired mind. In retrospect, I feel that it was about then we had reached the limit of our endurance, and nature in her own way, was making it easier for us to meet death.

The Esquimos were so pleased at our enjoyment of the fresh water that they suggested we stay there for our sleep. There were many excellent drifts of snow in the vicinity with which to construct a larger than average igloo to accommodate the six of us. We agreed wholeheartedly and without further ado, had soon constructed a veritable palace of an igloo. The Esquimos were travelling in comparative luxury, for they hauled out from their *komatik* armfuls of twigs and scrub with which they covered the floor of the igloo.

Before finally turning in, their last action was to unharness the dogs and feed them some of the frozen fish. The dogs then dug themselves into the deep snow for the night, despite the fact that the temperature must have been hovering around thirty degrees below zero. After we were all comfortably settled, out came the tea and Primus with which they were greatly impressed for they relied solely on water when on the trek. In true Esquimo fashion after having consumed the brew, they scooped out the leaves with their fingers and ate them with the greatest relish. We were also able to share with them our last remaining pieces of walrus, for their only food was fish. We retained a few pieces of the walrus for ourselves and cooked them over the Primus and seldom has meat tasted so delicious. The Esquimos, on the other hand, preferred their meat raw and the aroma of cooking meat held no attraction for them. In deference to them we consumed the fish they presented to us raw, but before it had a chance to thaw out.

The Esquimos, including the woman, were confirmed smokers and except when they were eating, never had their pipes out of their mouths. Terry and I had no inclination for tobacco having been without it for so long, but Bobby hauled out his pipe, accepted a fill and smoked it with the greatest relish. It was obviously chewing tobacco in its strongest form, jet black in appearance, and so hard that it took all their strength to cut it. After their pipes were pulling satisfactorily, we were obliged to reiterate our story over and over again and after each telling they appeared to become more and more astonished. Eventually we were so overcome by fatigue that we were obliged to excuse ourselves and soon fell into a deep sleep. We did not awaken until aroused by the Esquimos who were now ready with dogs harnessed and equipment packed for the final run to their settlement at Eclipse Harbour.

When we crawled out of the igloo there was a full moon and the night was wonderfully clear; seldom have I seen such a clear, bright night. The Esquimos were resolved to reach their destination without any more building of igloos or sleeps, only stopping periodically for short breathers and refreshments. With the greatest relief we were able to rid ourselves of our respective loads and place them on the *komatik*. It would not be possible for more than two to ride on the *komatik* at a time; the Esquimos insisted that Terry and I have the honour of being the first two. After about twenty minutes we jumped off and two others got on and so on. We progressed walking and trotting for about thirty or forty minutes, and riding for about twenty minutes. We travelled at least two hours in this manner before dawn broke, but yet another three hours elapsed before they decided to call a halt. It was the same place at which they had halted on the outward journey, for we were following their exact route and their tracks were still visible. It was now certain that barring accidents our next sleep would be at Eclipse Harbour. During this first short stop we made tea, but the kerosene was almost depleted and we decided to conserve the last drop for the last stop before making the final dash for the settlement.

The hectic *komatik* dash from moonlight to moonlight will forever stay in my memory, for it was moonlight again before we reached our destination. The poor dogs took a terrific beating, tired almost beyond endurance, with bleeding paws and frothing mouths, but the Esquimos were unconscious of it. To them dogs were merely a means of transportation and are not to be pampered. And so to the tune of alternate yelling from the Esquimos and howling from the dogs, we made our way up the coast.

It was not possible to adhere religiously to the coast; occasionally there would be a run inland, halfway up the side of a mountain when all would be obligated to push the *komatik* to reach the top. Then there would be the exciting dash down the other side when everyone jumped on board.

The poor dogs would take another beating with everyone yelling at them to go faster lest the *komatik* overtake them and spill us all into the snow. Although we almost capsized on several occasions, the Esquimos repeated this manoeuvre on every possible occasion and derived considerable fun and excitement out of it.

Freed of our loads, Terry and I experienced no difficulty in keeping up with the *komatik*. Strangely enough, we discovered that a steady trot was easier than walking when we became accustomed to it. Occasionally, the dogs would get the scent of some animal and despite their fatigue, would be off at top speed. That we had considerable difficulty in keeping up with. Unfortunately, we were never successful in finding anything to shoot, but these incidents provided a little excitement and served to increase our speed.

Just before darkness set in, when normally we would have called it a day, we made our final stop and finished our supply of kerosene by making tea. There was still a good supply of tea, which we resolved to present to the Esquimos when we arrived at their settlement. We rested for an hour, unharnessed the dogs, fed them, then were on our way again. We soon attained our original pace, which darkness did not interrupt, for the Esquimos were on familiar ground. Even the dogs knew their way, for they sped on hour and hour without hesitation. When the moon again showed itself, we felt a sense of real adventure mingled with excitement at the anticipation of meeting people again, for we knew that Eclipse Harbour was one of the largest Esquimo settlements on the coast.

We had been travelling for about three hours in bright moonlight and were descending a hill a short distance from the shore, when the dogs started howling in unison. Tired as they were, they dashed off at top speed as if they were just starting off on a trip instead of at the end of a most grueling one. The Esquimos informed us that our destination was just around a steep turn at the bottom of the hill. The dogs continued to gallop on ahead without hindrance from the Esquimos while we walked along slowly in the rear.

As we rounded the turn at the bottom of the hill, we came upon a village of igloos, the extent of which we were unable to judge in the waning moonlight. It appeared as if there were several parallel lines of igloos interconnected as if to permit access from one to another. Standing around were groups of Esquimo men and women, who when they heard the cries of the returning dogs, turned out to greet the hunters and inspect the spoils of the hunt, unaware that three strangers had been added to their company.

Bobby was now in his element, he was the lion of the hour, jabbering away at top speed to all and sundry. Especially to the women, who crowded around him obviously more interested in him as one of their own kind, then either Terry or me. When it was explained to them exactly who and what we were, they seemed to be immensely interested and regarded us more in the light of oddities than guests. Our appearance may have had a lot to do with it, for we did not realize at the time how odd we must have looked. When we arrived back at our base and looked into a mirror, we actually frightened ourselves. Terry and I were both reduced to skin and bone; my weight was only 125 pounds from an original 146 pounds. We were both very badly frostbitten about the face and hands. Our faces in particular were very sore and at times quite painful and were now almost covered with the dark brown scabs of healing frostbite.

After much chattering back and forth in a dialect strange to us, we were eventually introduced to the head man of the village who occupied the largest igloo and had the largest aggregate of women surrounding him. With Bobby as our interpreter, we repeated our story amid frequent interruptions of astonishment from the head man and those around him. After this he took us in hand and gave Terry and me each a wooden bunk constructed from driftwood on which to rest. Bobby had disappeared, obviously quite capable of looking after himself.

The igloos were not nearly as comfortable on the inside as they had appeared from the outside. The floors were inches deep in water caused by the melting snow as a result of the combined heat from so many bodies in such a confined space. To offset this, they had constructed duckboard tracks from driftwood and placed them around the floor. The igloos were inter-connected by low tunnels through which one was obligated to stoop quite low in order to pass. By comparison, the small igloos we were now accustomed to on our trek seemed infinitely more comfortable, with dry floors and not too warm in our snug sleeping bags. The large igloo we were now in was comfortless in appearance and uncomfortably hot, to the extent that the Esquimos, male and female alike, were beginning to discard their clothing while some were already in a state of complete nudity.

In this particular igloo, which was probably the most palatial in the village, the Esquimos slept on wooden bunks constructed from driftwood with skins for coverings. Terry and I were each provided with a very wide bunk, after which we handed out our tea requesting that they make some for us and then keep the remainder for themselves. They were childishly grateful for this negligible gift out of all proportion to its value. One of the women made herself busy preparing what to them was a distinct luxury. They had nothing so elaborate as a Primus stove for a source of heat, but their alternative, albeit primitive, was certainly most effective. They employed shallow pans from the Hudson Bay Co. filled with blubber fat, around the edge of which was placed moss gathered from between rocks. The moss was partially immersed in the fat and became an effective wick which emitted an excellent flame for light and heat, if kept properly trimmed. One of the chief duties of Esquimo women is to prepare and keep trimmed this type of lamp.

Several of these lamps were burning in this igloo with an Esquimo woman tending each one. On our request for tea, one of the woman produced a can from underneath a bunk, filled it with water from a barrel of thawing ice, and proceeded to boil the water over her blubber flame. When the water was boiling, she threw in a handful of tea and handed the can to us. The resultant brew was a trifle rugged, devoid of milk or sugar, but nevertheless most refreshing. After we had drunk our fill, we handed the can back to the woman who immediately polished off the tea leaves, smacking her lips with obvious relish. Cans were apparently at a premium, for this same one was used over and over again for successive brews. Each person, without fail, having consumed the brew, polished off the leaves before handing the can to the next consumer.

After this ritual was over, Bobby explained to the head man that white men preferred cooked fish to raw fish and proceeded to explain in detail how he had seen fish cooked at our base. The head man turned to one of the women and relayed these instructions; she immediately procured some water in the same can, placed some arctic cod in it and boiled it over one of the flames. It was one of the most delicious meals Terry and I had ever eaten. We enjoyed it so much that we asked for more, knowing full well that they were well supplied with fish. Our request pleased them immensely and was the best tribute we could have paid them. They continued to supply us with cooked fish until we could eat no more.

After about an hour, the women produced some flour from an obviously slender stock, mixing it with water and cooking it over a flame. The result was a kind of bannock loaf, which when eaten warm isn't too bad, but if allowed to cool, sets into a hard, dry paste. We promised that when we returned to our base we would send back enough flour to last them a long time.

In our weakened state the meal we had consumed had the effect of a seven course banquet and we now felt very sleepy. Expressing the wish that we turn in for the night, the Esquimos scurried around and produced several caribou and polar bear skins for us. I remarked to the head man that one of those wide bunks would suffice for both Terry and me, but he wouldn't hear of it. After a solemn conclave with several others, two very buxom ladies reported to me and two others, similarly buxom, reported to Terry. When we remonstrated to the head man, he solemnly explained that when the lamps went out during the night the igloo became quite cold, and we in our weakened state, would have difficulty in keeping warm. We were therefore to sleep between two of these ladies who would keep us nice and warm all night long. While this long explanation was taking place, the ladies had disrobed completely and were now quite naked. Without further ado, they climbed onto the bunks insisting that we lie between them, which we did with alacrity. This was done to the accompaniment of much bantering and merriment from the delighted Esquimos. It is sad to relate that in our weakened state we were unable to take full advantage of this interesting situation and fell unromantically fast asleep.

I was awakened from a very deep sleep in the middle of the night by one of my women climbing off the bunk onto the floor. To my consternation, she retrieved the one and only can from under the bunk and used it as we might a toilet bowl. I feverishly recalled that that was the very same can out of which I had recently consumed such delicious tea and boiled codfish. I particularity remembered that there was absolutely no effort made to wash or rinse it before using. While my mind was musing on this problem, my other lady companion entertained me in a similar manner, after which they both settled down again for the night without the slightest show of embarrassment. I did not get to sleep for quite a long time, during which several other women relieved themselves in like manner. The complete nonchalance with which this was carried out led me to believe that that was the primary purpose for which the can was intended.

I eventually got off to sleep again and slept soundly until awakened by the head man, who informed us that it was their objective to get us to our final destination as quickly as possible. We heartily agreed. Out came the can, and just as I thought, there was not the slightest effort to wash or even rinse it. It was simply dipped into the barrel of water and placed on the flame to boil. In the final analysis, boiling is as good a way as any to sterilize, so with this consoling thought, our breakfast of boiled fish and tea was consumed and enjoyed.

After we finished our meal we went outside and discovered that our hosts had ready a team of seven dogs and a large *komatik*. It was rather larger than the one we had been using the day before, perhaps with an eye to the supplies promised on our arrival back at our base. I questioned them as to the time it would take to reach Port Burwell and they informed me that normally it would take one sleep but this time they intended to run straight through with only short rests. This suited us admirably, for if we had stopped for a sleep we wouldn't have slept anyway.

To the accompaniment of loud chattering by the Esquimos and much barking and howling by the dogs, we bid our friends farewell. We promised to return and visit them with a *tingiook*, the Esquimo name for an aeroplane. And so we travelled, hour after hour, taking turns at riding and trotting. Moonlight gave way to darkness then darkness to dawn. We continued through the short period of daylight with occasional brief stops to rest the dogs and have a light refreshment. Just before darkness set in again we stopped for about an hour to unharness and feed the dogs and rest. Then off we were again into another night, into another full moon. About midnight, with the moon still bright, our goal came into sight. In the distance, across the bay, we could make out the Hudson Bay post. A little farther was the faint outline of the old Moravian Mission building, which was our home.

All was deathly quiet with not a soul astir. We wondered what the reaction would be like when we appeared, like dead men returned from the grave. As we neared, the base dogs acquired the scent of our dogs and set up a terrific howling. Although our dogs must have been tired to the point of complete exhaustion, off they went at a terrific pace we couldn't keep up with. Soon there were answering howls from the other dogs and altogether a veritable bedlam ensued. When we got within hailing distance, Bobby produced the rifle and fired our entire stock of forty-nine rounds into the air. The sound of firing produced an immediate reaction, the doors opened and out rushed everyone in various stages of undress. All were in utter amazement at our return from the dead. They completely overwhelmed us with their uncontrolled emotions at again seeing us alive and well. It will forever be an unforgettable moment in my life and one which cannot be adequately expressed in writing.

An immediate party was decided upon. We were physically carried into the dwelling and soon were relating our story over and over again, replying to question after question while our friends passed the liquor around. Terry and me with our empty stomachs, called it quits after one large brandy, but the others carried on into the night and during the rest of the next day. The official wireless operator, when he had heard sufficient of our story to make sense, dashed up to the transmitter and flashed the news over the air, both to Wakeham Bay, the base of expedition leader S/L T.A. Lawrence, and direct to Ottawa. Strangely enough, Ottawa received the news before Wakeham Bay, as they were on continuous watch. Wakeham Bay did not receive it until their next schedule, but on receipt of it, they immediately went on continuous watch. Bit by bit, they obtained the whole story which in turn was relayed to Ottawa. Soon the story was in the hands of the Canadian Press and was being relayed to newspapers all over the world.

CANADIAN PACIFIC RAILWAY COMPANY'S TELEGRAPH

TELEGRAM

CABLE CONNECTIONS TO ALL THE WORLD

J. McMILLAN, General Manager of Telegraphs, Montreal.

QTRAMR 18 RADIO RUSH MARCH 2-1928 STANDARD TIME.

PORT BURWELL VIA LOUISBURGNS NFT

MRS J LEWIS

    12 NORWOOD COURT WINNIPEGMAN (CARE TC WN)

YOUR HUSBAND HAS RETURNED AT MIDNIGHT TONIGHT STOP FURTHER TOMORROW

                COGHILL

1220A

Canadian Press

Los Angeles Times

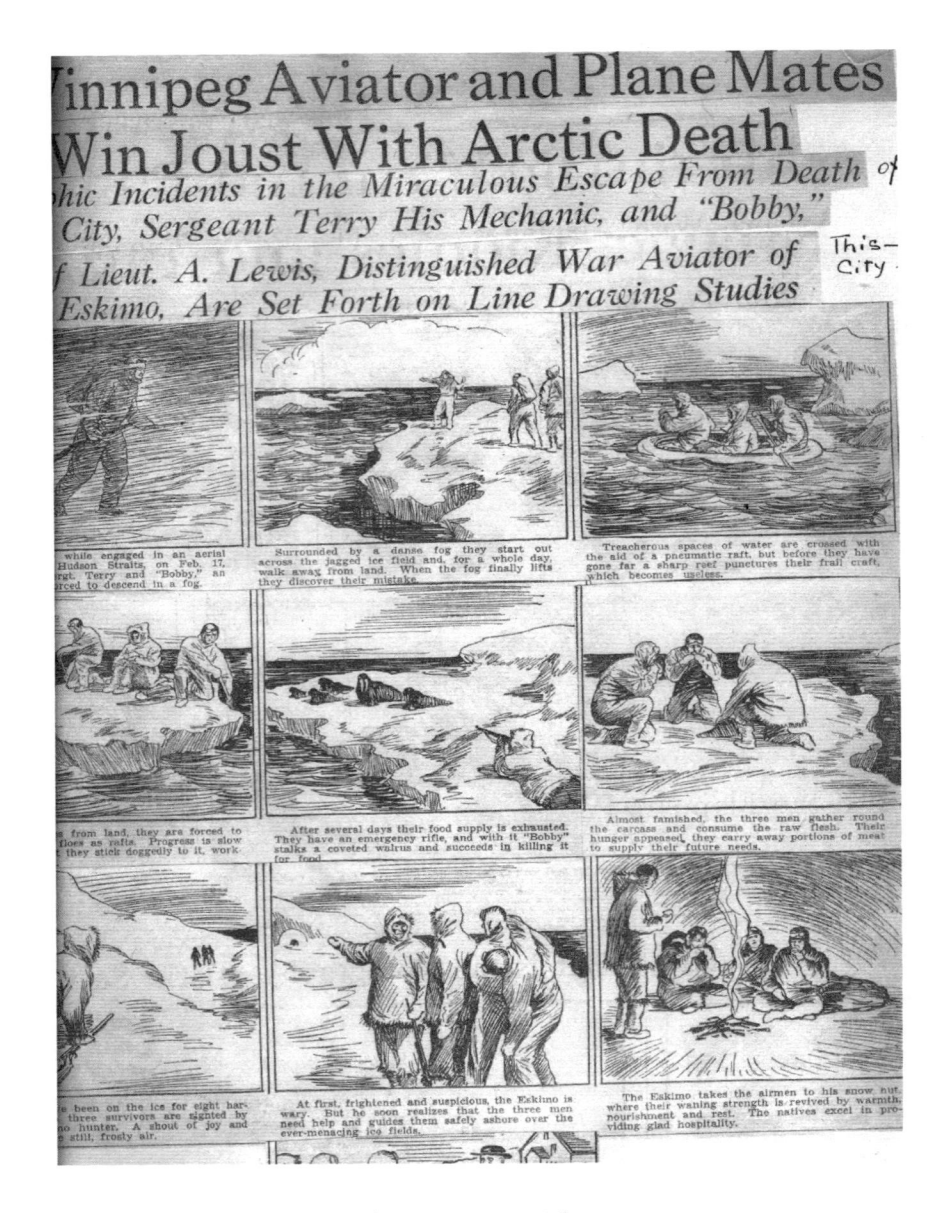

The Winnipeg Tribune

94   Pam McKenzie

MISSING AVIATORS SCAN HORIZON FOR POSSIBLE SIGHT OF RESCUERS

Latest reports to Canadian Air Defense officials indicate Flying Officer A. J. Lewis, Flying Sergt. N. S. Terry and "Bobbie", their Eskimo companion, were lost in the barren icefields of the Atlantic 16 1-2 days. It now being understood they were missing several days before any report was sent through to the capital. Official word, however, is awaited regarding the circumstances of their forced landing, due to a shortage of gasoline, previously reported to have been made February 17. It is believed the aviators lost their bearings while returning from a survey of the ice fields at the eastern end of Hudson straits, missed their base at Port Burwell and flew out over the Atlantic before being forced to land on the ice floe. It is not known whether the airplane was damaged in the landing or was icebound afterwards, but the trio were compelled to abandon it and indicate that salvage efforts would be futile. Details of what happened between the time of the landing and the subsequent arrival at the base are not available because the men were exhausted as a result of their battle against the elements and from hunger. Sufficient iron rations to last 12 days were taken, but these would have been exhausted long before the men reached safety. Firearms and a supply of ammunition also were taken, but it is not known whether they were successful in bagging any fowl, game or catching any fish. It is possible the airplane was dismantled to make fish hooks out of the wire stays and spears from the steel supports and the wooden framework to make fire. While they are recuperating at the Moravian Mission at Port Burwell the Canadian public just has received the graphic details of their rescue and return.

GRIPPING STORY BY LOST FLIERS

Vancouver Daily Province

    S/Leader Lawrence sent us a message that he was preparing to fly down from Wakeham Bay at first light to receive the story first hand. While the party was at its height, Dr. Kelly retrieved Terry and I and put us to bed in his own room where we should be safe from interruption. The sound of the celebration effectively prevented our sleeping however at least we were resting. He then received our story first hand so that he would be in a position to diagnose our condition and treat us accordingly.

We were immediately placed on a liquid and fish diet for at least a week and told we were to remain in bed for observation. After two days in bed a reaction set in and we found it was impossible to get out of bed without help. I well remember trying to get out of bed the first time; my head started spinning and I fell down onto the bed where I remained for the next few days.

We remained in bed for a week, closely watched by the doctor. He personally supervised every little thing we ate and did until he made up his mind that we had suffered no permanent ill effects. He then gave us a clean bill of health to get up and do as we pleased. During that week in bed we were obligated to retain our scraggly beards owing to the frostbite scabs. It was almost a month before we could have a proper shave. The brown scars remained for over a year and to this day one side of my face is extremely tender.

In the meantime, S/Leader Lawrence had arrived and had taken charge of the official reports and the transmission of them to Ottawa. To my joy, he informed me that he had decided to leave his aeroplane behind with us to replace the one I had lost. He would return to Wakeham Bay by dog team for the experience of the thing. With our experiences still fresh in our memory I didn't envy him his trip, but eventually he set out, and after weathering out two blizzards in igloos, he arrived back at his base in just under ten days.

Bobby all this while, was being feted royally by his own family in their own way; to do this they were issued with as many supplies of our stores as they wished. The two Esquimos who had brought us back home remained several days, taking part in the celebrations. When they were ready to return home, they were issued with as many stores as they could carry on the *komatik* and were promised still more if they cared to make a second trip. We were indeed sad to see those delightful people leave, for they had become almost as rescuing angels. They left us with the impression that we had been doing them a favour. Instead of accepting our thanks, which was offered from the bottom of our hearts, they were most profuse in extending theirs for the few supplies we had given them. This so-called civilization of ours could well profit by their example of sheer honesty, humility and simplicity.

The ambition of both Terry and me was to take an aeroplane over the entire route again to discover the exact spot where we had force landed. Therefore three weeks later we were up in the air again and across the Strait. On this particular occasion the weather conditions were perfect, extremely cold but with unlimited visibility in every direction. When we were halfway across the Strait we flew out into the Atlantic for about sixty miles, then south parallel to the Labrador, hoping to catch a glimpse of our aeroplane but with no luck. We flew down to Eclipse Harbour and flew over the Esquimo village at which we were guests. We would have landed had it not been that our fuel was running low and we were not quite sure of the landing conditions of the ice in that vicinity.

We had definitely been presumed dead, for an inventory had been taken of our personal kits and they had been packed in crates and roped ready for sending out with the first ship in summer. And so we resumed our former routine just exactly where we had left off.

Spring came very suddenly that year and the ice began breaking up earlier than in previous years. Soon the inlet at Port Burwell was suitable for operation off floats and we flew every day the weather permitted. I well remember my birthday the 15th of July, for on that day we had the worst blizzard of the year although the temperature was reasonably mild. This storm did more to break up the floes in the Strait than any previous storm, for immediately we noticed a change for the better. The wind was definitely the deciding factor as far as the ice conditions in our inlet were concerned. At times there would be open water as far as the eye could see, then overnight with a change of wind, the floes would be driven back onto the shore as if it were still the dead of winter.

And now, in the final analysis, what were the results of our long vigil? To begin with, the Strait never completely froze over owing to the strong current. The danger lay in the passage of ice floes down Fox Channel out through the eastern outlet into the Atlantic. This ice is tough, which even strong summer sun cannot melt but only reduce to large irregular chunks. By December 10th, the western end of the Strait was completely blocked by a huge pan stretching from the coast of Labrador to Nottingham Island. This date would therefore mark the last possible date on which navigation would be possible.

We recommended that July 15th should be the first possible date on which to commence navigation, but in the interests of safety, the end of July would provide a greater factor of safety. The fact remains that navigation in the Strait can be continued uninterruptedly for at least as long as navigation in the Great Lakes. The determination of this fact alone fully justified the expense of the expedition.

And so ends the Hudson Strait Expedition and the incredible survival story of Alexander Lewis.

PART THREE

Flight Lieutenant Alexander Lewis went to Britain in 1935 for two years, first with 13 (AC) Squadron flying Hawker Audax aircraft, then with 7(B) Squadron, which flew Handley Page Heyfords and the latest Armstrong Whitworth Whitleys capable of carrying two tons of bombs. F/L Lewis logged considerable day and night cross-country flying as well as bombing practice using both manual and automatic pilot procedures. This helped greatly when he returned to Canada and was given command of the RCAF's 3(B) Squadron in Ottawa. His training focus was long-range navigation and night flying.

In 1938, No. 3(B) Squadron moved from Ottawa to Calgary and began training with Wapiti aircraft – slow, obsolescent biplanes. The aircraft took off from Ottawa on Oct. 18, 1938, and took seven days to fly 2,300 miles due to weather delays. The ground party, travelling by train, beat the aircraft to Calgary by several days.

At the outbreak of the Second World War, Alexander Lewis was named to command one of Canada's bomber squadrons of twin-engine Lockheed Hudson aircraft, which swept over the Atlantic protecting and escorting convoys. He wrote of this experience:

> Everything in this world is purely relative, and what to some may appear hair-raising, to me now was merely routine. Anything that happened to me in the RCAF was a picnic in comparison with all that had happened before. Flying the squadron across the country when war broke out was strictly routine.
>
> During the war, the job I enjoyed most was ferrying Catalinas from Bermuda to Scotland and then returning by sea. This involved a non-stop 27-hour flight diagonally across the North Atlantic in the middle of winter. On one of these return trips by sea, our small 2,000 ton ship with two diesel engines, was accompanying a 10,000 ton ship en route to China with seven hundred passengers aboard. We were attacked by two Focke-Wulf Condors about six hundred miles off the west coast of Ireland. A stick of bombs was dropped on the larger ship and it started to sink immediately. Lifeboats were put

overboard laden with approx. fifty people each, some rafts without any oars. We were forced to witness lifeboat after lifeboat capsize in the mountainous sea and everyone aboard those boats were washed away. We were able to pick up about two hundred survivors half dead with exposure. One woman died in my arms bleeding to death from wounds and my greatcoat was drenched in blood.

One of the Condors had attacked us with cannon and practically demolished the bridge. Fortunately, our wireless was still working and when dawn broke a destroyer appeared alongside and escorted us back to Stornoway in the Outer Hebrides. We proceeded stern first most of the way using the emergency steering apparatus at the stern of the ship.

As the war raged on, an increase in bombing missions in Europe caused the demand for air observers to grow. The two Air Navigation Schools (ANS), in Rivers, MB, and Pennfield Ridge, NB, were merged into the Central Navigation School (CNS) in Rivers. This decision was made for economic reasons, as well as the belief that meteorological conditions in Manitoba were ideal for celestial navigation training.

The Standard PHOTONEWS, Nov. 18–25, 1939

Aim Of Older Pilots Is To Become Oldest

IF fortyish R.C.A.F. pilots go to bed early and keep away from liquor parties it's not because they're prudes and sissies.

It's because they've found that "partying" doesn't pay if one is an aeroplane pilot and if one wants to live to a ripe old age.

Forty-two-year-old Group Captain Alexander Lewis, commanding No. 1 Air Navigation school at Rivers, stated this belief when he spoke to a Canadian Club luncheon today in the Royal Alexandra hotel.

"We who are older have lost all ambition to be the BEST pilots in the R.C.A.F.—now we want only to be the OLDEST pilots in the R.C.A.F."

Two Don't Mix

"We have found out that one cannot become really merry too often and stay out late at night continuously, and still operate aeroplanes with the meticulous care and alertness needed to avoid accidents.

"Many of the younger pilots who spend their spare time partying would do well to learn this before it is too late."

The group captain described his experiences flying one of the first amphibians ferried to Britain from Bermuda.

There was not much thrill to it—"just extreme care, continual alertness and endurance. On the way he had seen two German submarines, forced them to crash-dive and reported their positions. He had spent all last winter in this service.

The Tribune, Winnipeg, Oct. 31, 1941

From 1941 to 1943, Group Captain Lewis commanded No.1 ANS then No.1 CNS in Rivers. By July of 1942, the staff at 1 CNS consisted of 103 officers, 1,932 airmen, and 248 civilians, with an additional 90 officers and 595 airmen as students. They operated 118 Avro Ansons and one Stinson HW-75 aircraft.

As reported in the *Winnipeg Free Press*, November 2, 1942:

> No.1 Central Navigation School at Rivers, MB, has trained hundreds of fliers who are now paving the way for victory by scientifically destroying the railroads and munitions plants of Germany. In almost every dispatch telling of the deeds of Allied airmen in bombing enemy territory, you find the name of a navigator who learned at Rivers to steer by the stars.
>
> Its Commanding Officer, Group Captain Alexander Lewis, a pioneer trans-Atlantic ferry pilot, is one of the Canadians who believed in victory through air power long before the idea became popular.
>
> The key plane in a chain of Allied bombers going to raid the Reich is the trail-blazer, the first plane which leads the others to the target and drops incendiary bombs to show the other planes where to put their block-busters. It is essential, Group Captain Lewis explained, that the navigator in the trail-blazer shall find the target so that the air bomber can drop his incendiaries on the right spot. The only way the navigator can do this and the only way in which he can guide the bomber home in bad weather is through steering by the stars. A plane which is 2,000 miles away from its base can find its position to within four miles by using the stars.

In 1943, Group Captain Lewis arrived in Summerside, PEI, to command the General Reconnaissance School (No.1 GRS). Established to address the need for pilots and navigators to work in general reconnaissance over the North Atlantic, the school initially built to accommodate a thousand people, grew to accommodate approximately two thousand. Pilots trained for nine weeks and navigators for four weeks. The first students flew in the twin-engine Avro Anson Mark I, which was gradually replaced by the Mark V. Over six thousand airmen trained at the No.1 GRS. Upon graduation, most were assigned to Coastal Command, which operated nearly every type of aircraft that engaged in anti-submarine warfare.

As the war fought to an end, Group Captain Alexander Lewis was awarded the Air Force Cross on Jan. 1, 1945. The citation read: This Officer is an exceptional pilot and by his personal example and ability to fly on all occasions in all kinds of weather is an inspiration to all those serving under him. He has successfully carried out many hazardous flights in a long flying career. His flying ability, devotion to duty, energy and leadership have been in a large measure responsible for the completion of the heavy monthly flying commitments at the station he commands. He had flown 4,680 hours, 800 as an instructor.

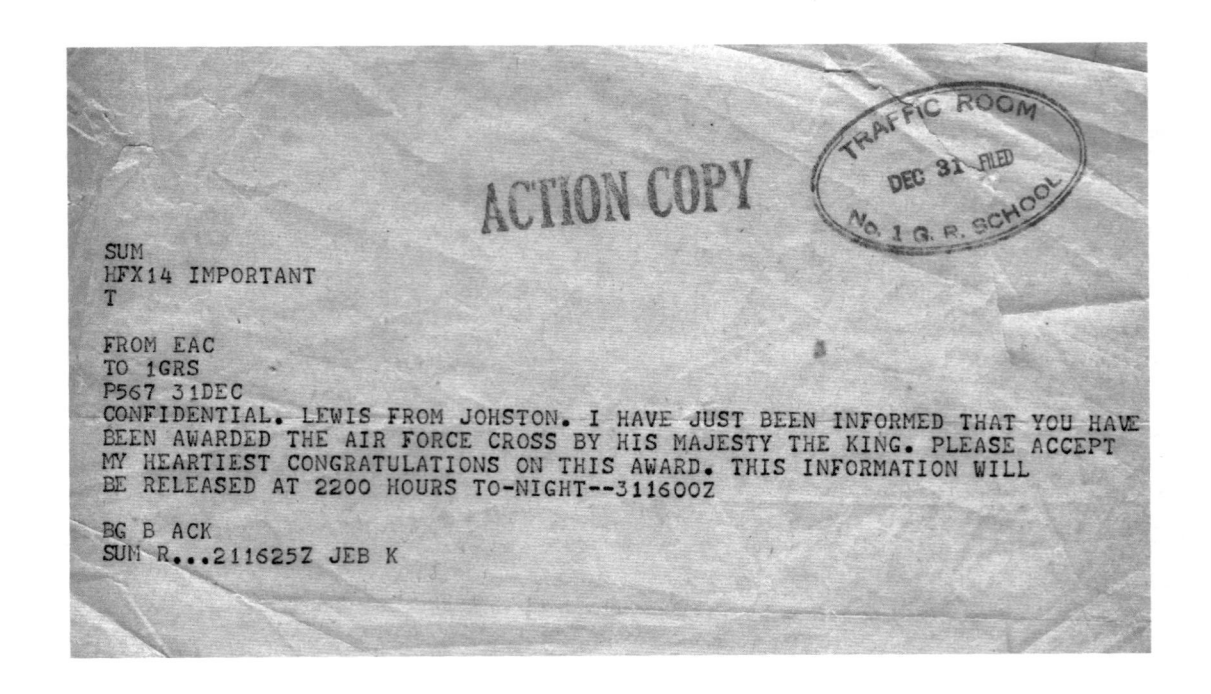

```
SUM
HFX14 IMPORTANT
T

FROM EAC
TO 1GRS
P567 31DEC
CONFIDENTIAL. LEWIS FROM JOHSTON. I HAVE JUST BEEN INFORMED THAT YOU HAVE
BEEN AWARDED THE AIR FORCE CROSS BY HIS MAJESTY THE KING. PLEASE ACCEPT
MY HEARTIEST CONGRATULATIONS ON THIS AWARD. THIS INFORMATION WILL
BE RELEASED AT 2200 HOURS TO-NIGHT--311600Z

BG B ACK
SUM R...211625Z JEB K
```

Photo credit: RCAF

Amid official testimonials of appreciation and gifts from the town of Summerside and area companies, G/C Lewis and Mrs. Lewis were transferred to RCAF Greenwood, NS, in Jan. 1946. His long and illustrious military career ended as Commanding Officer, RCAF Station Dartmouth, NS. He retired on Dec. 26, 1949.

Alexander and Jeanette Lewis relocated to Vancouver, BC.

Epilogue

IN DECEMBER 1924, Alexander Lewis became a Flying Officer and a charter member of the RCAF. He served continuously from that date until his retirement in 1949. His career was varied, but his interest in flying never wavered. His hobby was to fly as many different types of aircraft as possible and his ambition to fly to the last.

As detailed in nine original Pilot's Flying Log books, he reached his goal:

Aircraft Types Flown by Flying Officer Alexander Lewis

Armstrong Whitworth Atlas
Armstrong Whitworth Siskin
Armstrong Whitworth Whitley
Avro 100
Avro 504
Avro Anson Mk 1
Avro Anson Mk 5
Avro Avian
Avro Lynx
Avro Trainer
Avro Tutor
Avro Viper

Beechcraft Expeditor
Blackburn Shark
Boeing Stearman
Bristol Fighter
Bristol Tourer
Consolidated Catalina
Consolidated Courier
Consolidated Fleet
Consolidated Flying Boat PBY
Curtiss Fledgling
De Havilland Cirrus Moth
De Havilland Gipsy Moth

De Havilland Genet Moth
De Havilland Hawk Moth
De Havilland Mosquito
De Havilland Moth
De Havilland Puss Moth
De Havilland Tiger Moth
Douglas Dakota
Douglas Digby
Fairchild 2
Fairchild 51
Fairchild 71
Fairchild Seaplane
Fairey Firefly
Fairey Seaplane
Fleet 7
Fleet 80
Fokker Seaplane
Fokker Universal
Ford Tri-Motor
Handley Page Heyford
Hawker Audax

Hawker Tomtit
Lockheed Hudson
Lockheed Ventura
Noorduyn Norseman
North American Harvard
Northrop 17A
Reid Rambler [later Curtiss-Reid]
Royal Aircraft Factory R.E.8
Short 184 Seaplane
Stinson Voyager
Vickers Viking
Vickers Virginia
Westland Lysander
Westland Wapiti

Total: 59 Aircraft Types

On June 25, 1977, Mr. and Mrs. Lewis celebrated their Golden Wedding anniversary.

Group Capt. and Mrs. A. Lewis celebrate golden wedding.

Golden Wedding Celebrated

Friends and relatives called at the home of Group Capt. and Mrs. A. Lewis on Saturday, June 25 to honour them on the occasion of their golden wedding anniversary.

Alexander Lewis and Jeannette Cady met at Norway House in Manitoba and were married on Jaune 25, 1927 in Toronto.

Born in Bristol, England, Group Capt. Lewis saw service in the First World War as a member of the RFC that was later to become the RAF.

Following a period spent with Scotland Yard as an inspector in the special branch department, he came to Canada in 1924 and was taken on as a Flying Officer with the RCAF when it was still called the Canadian Air Board.

He saw service as a bush pilot in the Arctic and northern Manitoba and was in charge of an expedition over the Hudson Straits to determine the feasibility of opening a grain terminal at Churchill, Man.

Mrs. Lewis was born in Bernamwood, Wisconsin coming to Winnipeg in 1905, making her home there and later in the east.

Hostesses for the reception were Mrs. Lewis' sister, Mrs. Margurite Waterman, Mrs. M. Townsend, Lynda McKeie and Georgia Wilson.

Congratulations were received from Prime Minister Trudeau, Lieut-Governor Walter Owens Premier Bill Bennett, Human Resources Minister Bill Vander Zalm and MLA Graham Lea.

Alexander Lewis died on Dec 8, 1996 at the age of 97 years.
His storied life lives on in these pages …

Per ardua ad astra
Thorough difficulties to the stars

Endnotes/References

Adrift on Ice-floes: A Story of the Hudson Strait Expedition
Group Captain A. Lewis, RCAF
[Excerpts published in newspapers throughout the world in 1929]

Patrol Report No. A 24, February 17, 1928
Flying Officer A. Lewis

The Hudson Strait Expedition 1927–28
Wing Commander R.V. Manning, DFC, CD

Report of the Hudson Strait Expedition 1927–28
N.B. McLean, Officer in Charge

The Roundel
Royal Canadian Air Force, July 1949

Letter to Air Marshal C.R. Dunlap
Dated 5 February 1973

Printed in Canada